DIGITAL and MEDIA
LITERACY

For my first and best teacher, Rosemarie Shilcusky

DIGITAL and MEDIA LITERACY

CONNECTING CULTURE AND CLASSROOM

RENEE HOBBS

CORWIN
A SAGE Company

CORWIN
A SAGE Company

FOR INFORMATION:

Corwin
A SAGE Company
2455 Teller Road
Thousand Oaks, California 91320
(800) 233-9936
Fax: (800) 417-2466
www.corwin.com

SAGE Ltd.
1 Oliver's Yard
55 City Road
London EC1Y 1SP
United Kingdom

SAGE India Pvt. Ltd.
B 1/I 1 Mohan Cooperative Industrial Area
Mathura Road, New Delhi 110 044
India

SAGE Asia-Pacific Pte. Ltd.
33 Pekin Street #02-01
Far East Square
Singapore 048763

Acquisitions Editor: Carol Chambers Collins
Associate Editor: Megan Bedell
Editorial Assistant: Sarah Bartlett
Production Editor: Cassandra Margaret Seibel
Copy Editor: Tina Hardy
Typesetter: C&M Digitals (P) Ltd.
Proofreader: Dennis W. Webb
Indexer: Judy Hunt
Cover Designer: Michael Dubowe
Permissions Editor: Adele Hutchinson

Copyright © 2011 by Corwin

Printed in the United States of America

Library of Congress Cataloging-in-Publication Data

Hobbs, Renee.

Digital and media literacy : connecting culture and classroom / Renee Hobbs.

p. cm.
Includes bibliographical references and index.

ISBN 978-1-4129-8158-3 (pbk.)

1. Mass media in education—United States.
2. Media literacy—Study and teaching (Secondary)—United States.
3. Popular culture—Study and teaching (Secondary)—United States. I. Title.

LB1043.H627 2011
371.33'30973—dc22
2011007621

This book is printed on acid-free paper.

11 12 13 14 15 10 9 8 7 6 5 4 3 2 1

Contents

Online
Resources
Included

More online! Go to www.corwin.com/medialiteracy for
lesson plans, video clips, and discussion questions for
every chapter.

Preface

Virtually all aspects of the practice of education have their roots in effective communication.

Good communicators are open, active listeners. They bring a spirit of goodwill to their interactions with other human beings. They seek out opportunities to deepen understanding by asking good questions. They're curious and open to getting in over their heads in the search for knowledge. They avoid making snap judgments. They activate the mind, heart, and spirit in all their encounters with the people around them, listening and responding with the whole self to the other whole self they're interacting with.

Good communicators are self-aware. They ask questions in search of understanding. They're passionate about something that matters to them. They recognize their own values and needs and use advocacy to accomplish their goals and get things done.

Good communicators live in the present tense. They're awake to what's happening in the here and now. Sensitive to context, they take in each little nuance of the moment and adapt to it, moving with the flow. Good communicators try new things. They improvise. They play well in the sandbox with others. Good communicators are lifelong learners. Every good teacher I have ever met has these qualities.

If you've picked up this book, it's because you're interested in helping your students strengthen their critical thinking, collaboration, and communication skills, and you think that digital media, mass media, and popular culture may be useful resources and tools to support those goals.

Whether you're a school leader, teacher educator, curriculum specialist, technology teacher, or library/media specialist or teach English, social studies, health, science, business, video production, or the fine and performing arts, you'll find ideas in this book that help you make better use of media texts and technology tools. If you read this book and discuss it with your colleagues, you'll be able to work collaboratively to infuse digital and media literacy into your school's curriculum.

In this book, you'll find stories of teachers in Grades 7–12 who are connecting the classroom to the culture in their middle-school and high school English, history, chemistry, health, or video production courses. Principals, counselors, technology coaches, and library/media specialists play important roles in this book, too. Armed with a clear understanding of key concepts of digital and media literacy and its deep theoretical roots, these educators use powerful instructional practices to reach all learners.

Our students are swimming in an ever-changing world of media, technology, and popular culture. Social networking, music, movies, celebrities, athletes, and video games are key pleasures for young people around the world. There's just so much entertainment and information competing for our attention at all times of the day and night. And today, the scarce resource is human attention. In an age of information overload, learning to allocate one's attention to high-value messages is perhaps the one skill that will continue to reap benefits across the life span.

Every day of our lives, we create and consume messages using language, graphic design, images, and sound. We participate in social networks where sharing is valued as a form of personal expression and social learning. We manipulate a wide variety of types of symbols in both formal and informal settings, and these skills are now fundamental to the workplace. For the growing number of knowledge-economy jobs—from services including marketing and distribution as well as creative industries such as engineering and architecture—people need to be comfortable in manipulating symbols and using multiple digital platforms for collaboration and sharing.

The inclusion of digital and media literacy in secondary education promotes lifelong learning. Keep reading, and you'll learn about school leaders, technology and library/media specialists, and teachers in science, history, English, health, and other subject areas who have developed creative and effective strategies to bring digital and media literacy to learners. This book addresses these two questions:

- How can educators make use of popular culture, mass media, and digital technologies to help students develop *critical thinking skills?*
- How do students learn to be *responsible and effective communicators* with an appreciation of the human condition in all its complexity?

According to the Common Core Standards, just as media and technology are integrated in school and life in the 21st century, skills related to media use (both critical analysis and production of media) must be integrated into the curriculum across all subjects in secondary education.

In the Common Core Standards, we find the following statement:

> To be ready for college, workforce training, and life in a tech-nological society, students need the ability to gather, compre-hend, evaluate, synthesize, and report on information and ideas; to conduct original research in order to answer ques-tions or solve problems; and to analyze and create a high volume and extensive range of print and nonprint texts in media forms old and new. The need to conduct research and to produce and consume media is embedded into every aspect of today's curriculum. In like fashion, research and media skills and understandings are embedded throughout the Standards rather than treated in a separate section.

In this book, I show how digital and media literacy offers the potential to reinvigorate both the arts and humanities and the natural and social sciences in Grades 7–12. By helping students and teachers use creative and powerful ideas that bring relevance to the classroom, students explore contemporary culture, media, and technology as they build communication and critical thinking skills. As you explore how mass media, popular culture, and digital media can be used to support academic achievement, you'll get ideas from this book that you can put directly into action.

Publisher's Acknowledgments

Corwin gratefully acknowledges the contributions of the following reviewers:

Melody L. Aldrich, English Teacher and Department Chair
Poston Butte High School
San Tan Valley, AZ

Abbey S. Duggins, Instructional Coach
Saluda Educational Complex
Saluda, SC

Patti Grammens, Eighth-Grade Physical Science Teacher and Science
    Department Chair
Lakeside Middle School
Cumming, GA

Kay Kuenzl-Stenerson, Literacy Coach
Merrill Middle School
Oshkosh, WI

Shannon Shilling, Sixth- and Seventh-Grade Language Arts Teacher
Fort Riley Middle School
Fort Riley, KS

John Shoemaker, Technology Program Specialist
Department of Educational Technology
School District of Palm Beach County
West Palm Beach, FL

Michelle Strom, Language Arts Teacher
Fort Riley Middle School
Fort Riley, KS

About the Author

 **Renee Hobbs** is one of the nation's leading authorities on digital and media literacy education. She has created numerous award-winning videos, websites, and multimedia curriculum materials for K–12 educators and offers professional development programs to educators in school districts across the United States. Her research examines the impact of media literacy education on academic achievement and has been published in more than 50 scholarly and professional books and journals. She is a professor at the School of Communications and Theater at Temple University in Philadelphia, where she founded the Media Education Lab (http://www.mediaeducationlab.com). She received an EdD from the Harvard Graduate School of Education, an MA in Communication from the University of Michigan, and a BA with a double major in English Literature and Film/Video Studies from the University of Michigan.

ACCESS

1

Why Digital and Media Literacy

What You'll Find in This Chapter:

- Students' at-home media use habits are generally unknown to their teachers.
- Young people need opportunities to engage with adults in making sense of the wide variety of experiences they have with mass media, popular culture, and digital technologies.
- Teachers' own love–hate attitudes about print, visual, sound, and digital media shape their uses of media and technology in the classroom.
- A process model for digital and media literacy includes these components: access, analyze, compose, reflect, and take action.
- Learners thrive when teachers move beyond the textbook to include real-world texts in a wide variety of forms.

Lesson Plan:

Four Corners on the Media: Reflecting on Our Love–Hate Relationship

When Tony's not in school, he's on the computer. And when he's not playing video games or doing his homework, he's watching Hulu. "It's great to be able to watch your favorite shows whenever you want," he explained. These days, he's been watching the first two seasons of *Greek*, an ABC comedy about a girl who navigates her way through a sorority at an Ohio university. Her party life is turned upside down when her younger brother arrives on campus and insists on rushing a fraternity.

But Tony doesn't just watch TV shows online; he "reads the boards." All the shows on Hulu have a discussion board, where people make comments and participate in discussion about issues related to each show. He's posted his two cents on the longstanding debate about the sex jokes on *Family Guy*. He's clarified a plot point or two on the *Bones* discussion board, answering people's questions about why a character acted a certain way. Now he's got something to add to the board about why *Greek* doesn't seem like it's set in Ohio:

Figure 1.1   Discussion Board for ABC Family's *Greek*

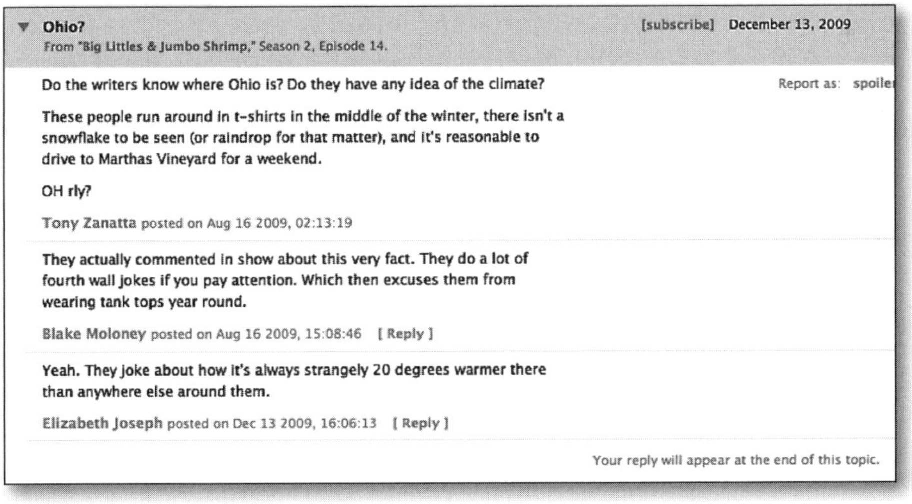

One thing is clear: Tony is no couch potato. He has analyzed some elements that make the show unrealistic, as shown in Figure 1.1, and he's active in an online conversation with others who have strong opinions about the show. By reading reactions to his post, Tony can learn from other users about concepts like the *fourth wall*, which refers to the boundary between any fictional setting and its audience. When actors speak to the audience directly through the camera in a television program or film, it is called "breaking the fourth wall."

Tony's high school English teacher would be pleased to see Tony engaged in this kind of literacy practice. She works hard to get her students to appreciate literary concepts in epic poetry and mythology. But she doesn't generally spend time talking with students about their favorite movies or TV programs. She is too busy covering all the classic works of literature that students read in college prep classes.

As it turns out, many teachers are unfamiliar with how students actually watch movies and television today. Kids are using video streaming websites like Netflix (www.netflix.com) or Hulu (www.hulu.com). Netflix not only will mail movie DVDs to your door, but it offers video streaming direct to your computer or to your TV through an Xbox or Wii video game system. Hulu was founded in 2007 as a collaborative venture between FOX, ABC, and NBC. It offers television programs to viewers online through an advertising-supported model. Videos are available for unlimited streaming. In the United States, people can watch favorite shows and edited video clips over and over, for free. Advertisements appear during normal commercial breaks. For teens, it's the second most popular website destination (after YouTube) in terms of minutes of use.[1] And most teens use Hulu to rewatch their favorite episodes of shows they've already seen on TV.

What's to love about ABC's *Greek?* Tony explains it this way: "The characters are likeable and complicated—at least the male characters. And some of these stories show you what college life is like, even if the comedy elements add a lot that's unrealistic. The clothes and appearance of the characters are definitely not realistic."

What's to hate about watching this show? Tony admits, "I like watching them in a marathon session. Sometimes, it's really not a great use of my time." Like many people, Tony plays video games and watches TV instead of doing the things he *should* be doing, like homework and chores. "I waste a lot of time this way," he smiles sheepishly. When Tony's done watching episodes of *Greek,* a computer algorithm on Hulu suggests other shows he might also enjoy watching, including *The Secret Life of the American Teenager, Ten Things I Hate About You,* and *Ugly Betty.* Of course, Tony and his friends are also listening to music, playing video games, watching

YouTube videos, updating their social networks, and using cell phones. But for about four hours and twenty minutes per day, it's TV viewing on a traditional set, usually in the bedroom.

The Uses of Media and Technology in Grades 7–12

Many teachers already use movies, videos, mass media, and popular culture in the classroom. In middle-school health class, a Discovery Channel video on nutrition helps kids understand how food choices affect health. In world history classes, a teacher may show clips from *The Gladiator* or *300* to discuss Greek and Roman warrior culture or examine how the film's visual depictions of the ancient world compare with what is known from written historical accounts. In English, a teacher may use lyrics from a pop song to help students understand meter in poetry or a clip from *The Simpsons* to explore the concept of intertextuality. In biology, a PBS documentary on the Amazon basin may help spark interest in the genetic diversity of species. In government class, teachers may use an episode of *Law and Order* to discuss the dangers of pretrial publicity.

Computers are used in widely different ways in American schools. Students may go to the computer lab when writing their research papers. They may use drill-and-practice software to learn math or play educational simulation games to explore global conflicts in Latin America or the Middle East. In some schools, students are using computers as an ordinary part of classroom learning. But while plenty of teachers use digital media, mass media, and popular culture in the classroom, the instructional strategies they use may (or may not) support the development of students' knowledge, critical thinking, and communication skills.

Sometimes digital technology is used as a babysitter. There's the teacher who lets kids bring in DVDs from home to watch on the Friday before the holiday. There's the one who takes her kids to the computer lab for a project but doesn't notice when they're distracted and off task. Then there's the one whose classroom is always darkened, with a movie screening and kids' heads on desks.

Now there's a topic teachers don't like to talk about. In American public schools, for over two generations, watching movies has long been used *as a break or a reward*. These practices are so typical and so ordinary that we take them for granted. But in some schools, watching videos can become a crutch: it can be used as a way to fill time and keep students in their seats. In my work with teachers, I've found that these habits may interfere with developing more imaginative and innovative uses of media and technology for learning.[2]

Other educators use popular culture as a motivational bait and switch, a way to get bored and disengaged youth to gear up for digging into *King Lear.* For example, a business teacher might use clips from the film *Wall Street* to introduce ideas about risk and return in finance. A math or science teacher may use a clip from the CBS show *NUMB3RS* to help students see the wide-ranging impact that math can have on their daily lives. A physical education teacher might "warm up" a class by playing some pop music to get kids moving. In nearly any subject, a clip from a YouTube video or talking about Oprah, local sports, or *World of Warcraft* can get kids to pay attention at the beginning of class. And who doesn't sometimes leave the substitute teacher a movie to play in class?

Make no mistake about it: using popular culture, mass media, and digital media motivates and engages students. And students need to be motivated and engaged—genuine learning simply doesn't happen without it. But this book isn't about simply using superficial strategies for getting kids to pay attention. Instead, this book explores the truly transformative power of digital and media literacy education in Grades 7–12 to connect the humanities, natural sciences, and social sciences to mass media, digital media, and contemporary culture.

The position paper on digital and media literacy developed by the National Council for the Social Studies (NCSS) explains that changes in society challenge teachers to change both how and what we teach:

> Whether we like it or not, this media culture is our students' culture. Our job is to prepare them to be able to critically participate as active citizens with the abilities to intelligently and compassionately shape democracy in this new millennium. Media literacy offers us the framework to build upon their entertainment and social experiences with media so as to provide our students with meaningful academic, civic, and public experiences that are critical and empowering.[3]

Educators can't afford to ignore or trivialize the complex social, intellectual, and emotional functions of media and popular culture in the lives of young people. In order to reach today's learners, educators need to be responsive to students' experience with their culture—which is what they experience through television, movies, YouTube, the Internet, Facebook, music, and gaming.

When you learn more about students' choices, the first thing you'll notice is how different your students are from you. When it comes to media and technology, every two years brings a new set of changes in the landscape of their daily life. Even if you're only a few years older than your students, there may be important differences because technology tools are changing so very rapidly. That's why educators need to gain the latest information about the media and technology choices students make at home (and at school) each day.

Understanding Today's Learners

Kids are using media and technology from before breakfast until bedtime and beyond. They're sending text messages, listening to music, updating their social media profiles, and playing video games at the same time, squeezing in 200 hours of media and technology use into each month.[4] Contrary to popular opinion, most teens ages 12 to 19 are *not* abandoning movies and television for the Internet; when they go online, they're updating their Facebook profiles and watching YouTube videos but generally not creating videos, blogs, podcasts, or computer programs. Only 8% of teenagers use Twitter, for example.[5] Despite all the attention given to teens and online media in the news media, television programs and movies continue to be significant sources of entertainment in the lives of young people. A Nielsen study in June 2009 shows that only about 3% of the 100 hours per month that teens spend using television is done online. Actually, teens watch more TV than ever, up 6% over five years. And teens actually spend about one third less time online as compared with adults, using the Internet about 11 hours a month as compared with adults, who spend 29 hours monthly online.[6]

Way back before cable television and online video streaming brought us a 500,000-channel universe, it was easy for 20th-century teachers to integrate discussions of favorite TV shows into the classroom—after all, there were only three or four networks. Back then, discussions about mass media emerged naturally as a result of shared exposure to celebrities, politicians, athletes, and musicians. Of course, teachers still have viewing experiences they can share with their students. Many teens and teachers love *American Idol*, for example. Both teens and teachers may watch sports as well as local and national news.

But today, the media worlds that students inhabit are often very different from the preferences of educators, parents, and other adults. Teachers and students are both "using the Internet," but they are having very different experiences when online. When teachers use the Internet, for example, it's often to check e-mail or surf the web for information related to career, health, or hobbies. When teens use the Internet, the purpose is for socializing or entertainment, generally by playing games, watching videos, searching for and listening to music, and interacting with friends through social networks like Facebook or Myspace.

As important as digital media and technology are in the lives of children and young people, research shows that 80% of teens have little to no interaction with parents or other adults about their use of media and technology.[7] So most young people get very little opportunity to have serious conversations with adults about the complex mix of entertainment, socialization, and information that is a substantial part of everyday life.

But it is through digital media, mass media, popular culture, and technology that we will get most of our information and entertainment across the span of a lifetime. Shouldn't students get some meaningful opportunities to analyze and evaluate the way these messages and experiences work in contemporary culture?

Keep a Media Diary

Increase your awareness of each time you come in contact with print, visual, sound, or digital media for a three-day period. You can create your own method for keeping track of your usage habits, but please note the following:

- Type of media text (print, visual, sound, or digital)
- Title or name of the media text
- Amount of time spent using it
- Motivation for using it (homework, socializing, relaxation, mood management, etc.)
- Context and situation (where and why)

After three days, review the chart to look for patterns. Write a short essay describing the patterns and reflect on your thoughts and feelings regarding media use choices over this period of time. In the essay, address these questions:

1. What medium do you use the most? What do you use the least? Why?

2. Was your media use during this period of time more or less typical for you? Why or why not?

3. Reflecting on your behavior over the three-day period, which medium could you live without, if necessary? Which medium would be most difficult to live without? Why?

4. Which types of media do you use as part of a social activity and which are used mostly when you are alone? What factors explain this?

5. How do you use different types of media for work, social communication, and leisure purposes?

6. Is there anything about your consumption of media that you would like to change? Why or why not?

Our Love–Hate Relationship With Media and Technology

The word *media* has only been used to refer to communication since the 1920s, when it started to be used as the plural form of *medium*, which was used to mean "an intervening agency, means, or instrument." The term was first applied to newspapers, then radio, and then television. Now we use it to include many types of digital communication, including websites, e-mail, and social networking. (Because it's a plural form, we say, "Media are. . . .") These days, media are usually categorized in four formats: print, visual, sound, and digital media, as shown in Figure 1.2.

Figure 1.2   Types of Media

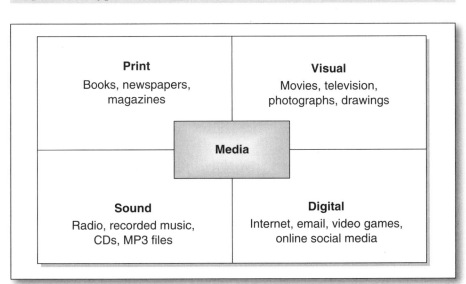

Categories for defining media types have become blurry as more and more of our media are expressed in digital forms. For example, an audio book represents the convergence of print, sound, and digital media forms. Online social media bring together elements of both mass communication and interpersonal communication. Every day, it seems, there are new digital media resources and tools that attract the interest of K–12 educators. That's because a vast network of designers and creative professionals are generating lots of new tools for online media, hoping to change the world or just strike it rich (by creating the next Facebook, Wikipedia, or even just a new puzzle video game for the cell phone, like Angry Birds). Some of these new tools have enormous potential for education. For example, Voice Thread (www.voicethread.com) is a way to collaboratively comment on images. Jing (www.jingproject.com) is a tool that lets you make a digital file of still or moving images on your computer screen. Every week, new products and services are being introduced for use at home, too. For some educators, being first to use a new technology tool is a personal obsession. For many others, this holds little attraction or appeal.

But because we use many types of media routinely as part of everyday life, most people have a love–hate relationship with print, visual, sound, and digital media and technology. These perspectives come from our roles as individuals, as parents, as educators, and as citizens. And because our attitudes about media and technology will inevitably shape our decisions about using media in the classroom, it's important to reflect on our own beliefs and attitudes and consider what matters most to us.

Were Tony to interview his teacher and her school colleagues about their attitudes about digital media and technology, he might find these diverse views:

- Print media are superior to digital media.
- Cell phones are like having a computer in your pocket.
- The celebrities and athletes we see in mass media are a form of cultural glue that holds our society together despite our different backgrounds.
- Digital technology lets anyone be an author!
- Media and technology firms are giant corporations just out to make money.
- Cell phones are essential today, but they do interfere with real life.

- Making your life public on Facebook makes you feel like a celebrity.
- Media are a tool of political power: By controlling information and entertainment, you control the world.

Add your own ideas to this list. Now consider what a great variety of perspectives are possible. There's no doubt about it: Teachers' attitudes about media and technology shape their curriculum choices. Who would be surprised to find that a teacher who views media as an art form would make different use of movies, newspapers, or websites in the classroom than one who is convinced that the Internet is going to revolutionize the world, or another who sees mass media as a tool of political control, or another who thinks it's just a form of superficial entertainment?

At the end of this chapter, you'll find a lesson plan to unpack how your own students understand their love–hate relationship with print, visual, sound, and digital media.

Students have lots of things to say about this because media and technology are so important to them. Some are using genres and formats that many of their teachers and parents don't even recognize (web comics, discussion boards like 4chan, and fake Wikipedia sites, for example). Some teens will have thought deeply about media and technology in terms of the positive and negative functions, while others just take it all for granted.

When teachers and students are asked to reflect on their perspectives to prioritize the dimensions of their relationship with print, visual, sound, and digital media, they clarify their values. Such reflection is a vital part of participating in contemporary society today, and it is the first step in the pedagogy of digital and media literacy education.

Essential Dimensions of Digital and Media Literacy

In this book, you'll meet middle-school and high school teachers, principals, library/media specialists, and technology educators from all across the United States, people that I have had the privilege to know over the course of my career. By sharing my experiences observing in their classrooms, interviewing them, and reviewing their students' videos, writing, multimedia, websites, and other creative work products, I hope to illustrate the complexity, depth, and richness of the practice of digital and media literacy in secondary education. To organize the many different types of instructional practices, I present a process model for digital and media literacy that emphasizes five communication competencies as fundamental literacy practices that are now part of learning across all the subject areas.[8] The essential dimensions of digital and media literacy include these five elements:

1. **ACCESS.** Finding and sharing appropriate and relevant information and using media texts and technology tools well.

2. **ANALYZE.** Using critical thinking to analyze message purpose, target audience, quality, veracity, credibility, point of view, and potential effects or consequences of messages.

3. **CREATE.** Composing or generating content using creativity and confidence in self-expression, with awareness of purpose, audience, and composition techniques.

4. **REFLECT.** Considering the impact of media messages and technology tools upon our thinking and actions in daily life and applying social responsibility and ethical principles to our own identity, communication behavior, and conduct.

5. **ACT.** Working individually and collaboratively to share knowledge and solve problems in the family, the workplace, and the community, and participating as a member of a community at local, regional, national, and international levels.

This five-part process is fundamental to how we learn and communicate today. One metaphor for digital and media literacy is to consider it as a huge constellation of stars in the universe: Each star reflects different skills, habits of mind, and competencies. But because this literacy constellation is so vast, educators often focus on just one part of the universe. Or else they may paint a picture of the whole night sky in a once-over-lightly fashion. As I see it, the digital and media literacy universe has five distinct dimensions that spiral together in an interconnected way.

The Access Dimension:
Using, Finding, and Comprehending

Access is the first step in literacy—learning how to find, comprehend, and use symbolic resources. In preschool, we may sometimes need to teach a basic access skill for using books. For example, we teach children how to hold books, open them, turn the pages, and notice the relationship between the words and pictures. Decoding printed words into meaning through comprehension is another kind of access skill.

Access is always media-specific: each media form has a distinctive group of things you need to know in order to make sense of it. When it comes to using a computer, there are numerous such kinds of basic competencies involved. For example, to contribute to a wiki or blog, people need to understand file management, how to edit, and how to use formatting tools. To find information online, there's another set of specific skills, including generating appropriate keywords and selecting appropriate search engines. To participate in online social networks, you may need the ability to interact socially using avatars, or the ability to adapt material from one context and use it in another, or to use multitasking to get things done. And while you may be able to acquire some of these access skills on your own (just by messing around), you'll go farther with a knowledgeable person nearby, available to help you out when needed.

Consider how access competencies are part of your curriculum:

- *Using technology tools.* Do students get to use technology tools for finding information, problem solving, self-expression, and communication? Do assignments progressively deepen their capacity to use tools well? Or is going to the technology lab simply a matter of following directions on a worksheet? Or worse, is it a break from real learning?
- *Gathering information.* Do you model effective strategies for finding information from diverse sources? Do you give students opportunities to work independently? Do you give students choices? Or do you make most of the selections on their behalf?
- *Comprehending.* Are students challenged to make sense of texts? Do you create a learning climate where students' multiple interpretations are respected, valued, and shared? Or do you do most of the work of interpreting and explaining?

These skills embody the new Common Core Standards where research activities and information texts are emphasized, both through short, focused projects and longer-term activities. But the access dimensions of digital and media literacy can be intimidating. People can't be experts at everything. Library media specialists are masters of online database searching tools. Many social studies teachers know how to find historical documents using online archives. Most English teachers have mastered the finer points of word processing software. The technology teacher often knows how to use a lot of different software tools for creating websites and sharing ideas.

But don't ever feel guilty or inadequate about access skills you have or the skills you lack. There's no way most of us can keep up with the changing pace of technology. Most of us tend to learn the access skills we need to use on a day-to-day basis. Feelings of guilt and inadequacy may contribute to the kind of avoidance that can discourage exploration and experimentation. Since that's the case, both teachers and students need time to play with new tools, messing around and exploring so that they can continue to develop particular access skills when they need them.[9]

Analyze: The Critical Thinking Dimension

An important dimension of the literacy universe is the capacity to analyze messages, considering the author, purpose, and point of view to understand how they are constructed and the assumptions that underpin them. When we evaluate, we consider the value and worth of ideas by reflecting on them within a social, political, historical, economic, and cultural context. Canadian high school teacher Rick Shepherd talks about helping students develop an informed, critical understanding that involves examining the techniques, technologies, and institutions involved in media production; being able to critically analyze media messages; and recognizing the role audiences play in making meaning from those messages.[10]

Good questions are key to stimulating analysis and evaluation competencies. But vocabulary and background knowledge are also needed to situate knowledge and ideas within various contexts. For example, consider a teacher who is exploring the essential question: Why do humans share stories?[11] To get at this question, students might analyze a recent news story like Google's decision to digitize library books to make out-of-print books more widely available. To do this, it would help to have a solid understanding of the role of technological change in the publishing industry, the cultural and economic structure that has made Google so profitable, and even the relevant provisions of copyright law.

A different teacher might take on the same theme of why humans share stories and use it to analyze the spoken word movement in hip-hop poetry. To accomplish this, a good understanding of the characteristics of performance art would come in handy. Knowledge about the golden era of rap and the role of artists like Public Enemy and De La Soul would support practices of musical analysis. It could even be useful to know about the earliest traditions in spoken word poetry: Homer, the famous poet of ancient Greek culture.

As is obvious, the more we know, the deeper our questioning becomes, and the more likely that our analysis and evaluation will lead to gaining new information through a path of interrelated questions and discoveries. It is this fundamental process that leads to the creation of new knowledge.

Consider how analysis and evaluation competencies are part of your curriculum:

- *Asking good questions.* Do you ask open-ended questions that have no right or wrong answers? Do students' answers matter in your classroom? Do their questions matter?
- *Gaining knowledge.* Do your assignments and activities promote curiosity? Do students get to apply and use the knowledge they are gaining? Or is this knowledge mostly just a matter of memorizing what's needed to pass high-stakes tests?
- *Contextualizing.* Have you framed your curriculum around an essential question, one that touches hearts and souls, one that helps to define what it means to be human? In doing this, do students get to explore how political, social, economic, and cultural contexts shape the way we send and receive messages? Or are students only vaguely aware of the value of what they are learning?

Some educators shy away from activities that involve analyzing and evaluating because these competencies inevitably involve issues of *values and ideology.* The practice of analysis always has an embedded point of view. When teachers' values are substantially the same as the school and community values, this isn't generally a problem. But when teachers work in communities where families have values that are different from their own, analysis and evaluation practices can activate students' questioning in ways that make some parents and school administrators uncomfortable.

For example, in some communities, parents and teachers may have a shared concern about how materialistic values lead some young people to be obsessively concerned about brand names and other status symbols. But in other communities, a focus on the negative consequences of materialism might be seen as un-American or even elitist and snobby.

There's no doubt about it: A focus on analysis and evaluation is an essential part of the reading process, because as Robert Scholes explains, it enables students "to situate a text, to understand it from the inside sympathetically, and to step away from it and see it from the outside, critically."[12]

Communicate: The Expressive Dimension

Today, the shape of writing has changed, as students compose for meaningful purposes and real audiences, not just to complete a homework assignment, explains Troy Hicks, author of *The Digital Writing Workshop*.[13] Young people are composing on computers, and they are using video, sound, and interactivity. English teachers must help students pay attention to the discourse norms that exist in different contexts and communities. For example, students can learn that it's OK to use smiley emoticons when sending an e-mail thank you note to Aunt Laura but not OK to use them when writing an e-mail to the school principal.

Digital composition is also increasingly collaborative, as teams work together to conceptualize, rehearse, perform, and edit elaborate video productions that require people with a range of different talents and abilities.

Rhetoric is the term generally used to describe the process of helping students to speak and write effectively. Today, we can see how the principles of rhetoric are at work in helping students to acquire *textual power*, a term used by Scholes to describe the interconnection between analysis, evaluation, and composition.

Every teacher must consider how communication and composition are part of their teaching goals:

- *Expression in multiple modes.* Do students get to use different genres, including narrative, persuasive, and expository forms? Do they get to use image, language, sound, graphic design, performance, and interactivity to get their message across?
- *Authentic audiences.* Do students get to use literacy practices in ways that are meaningful forms of communication? Do they

"talk back" to texts? Or do they primarily summarize and reproduce the ideas they encounter? Does their work reach real audiences, or is it created as an exercise for the teacher to grade and return?

- *Content and form in relation to purpose and audience.* Do students get to shape a message's content based on their purpose and intended target audience? Or do students learn only standard forms, like the lab report, the research paper, the worksheet, or the five-paragraph essay?

Reflect: The Social Responsibility Dimension

All communication involves ethical and social values. We are constantly making choices about how to treat people whenever we interact socially. We are aware of how other's expectations for us may shape our own behavior. Nearly every secondary educator has heard stories about or personally experienced adolescents who may have made some poor choices when it comes to texting and social media. And even with school filters, some students manage to find ways to play online games in the computer lab on the sly, when the teacher's not looking. Throughout life, we all make choices whether or not to apply social responsibility and ethical principles to our own identity, our communication behavior, and our conduct.

Today, the Internet creates complex new ways for people to interact socially. Some characteristics of digital media—the instantaneousness, for example—may encourage impulsive behavior. A student may take a picture of a friend, and when he sees that the picture looks stupid (perhaps the kid has one eye closed and one eye open), impulsive action may lead to the photo being shared on Facebook. And because it's sometimes difficult to predict the consequences of an action, the student may find that the photo has been interpreted in many different ways. The friend may be annoyed, angry, or delighted. Others who see it will make their own judgments, too.

Privacy, copyright, fair use, attribution, and new forms of sharing offer other opportunities for rich conversations about ethical issues. Issues of representation come into play when people use digital images of themselves and their peers to represent their personal and social experiences. There's no doubt about it: What we do online affects our identity, our self-esteem, our relationships, and our future.

Teachers can support students' ethical, social, and emotional development when they do the following:

- *Encourage multiperspectival thinking.* Do students get to imagine the thoughts, feelings, and ideas of others? Are they encouraged to move beyond either–or thinking? Do they get safe opportunities to share their feelings and listen to others? Do they practice building empathy by reflecting on the experience of standing in someone else's shoes?
- *Predict consequences and use hypothetical reasoning.* Do students get to investigate the genuine conflicts they experience each day in the world outside the classroom? Do they get to apply reasoning skills to the challenges of daily life, especially in relation to communication and social relationships?
- *Talk about power and responsibility.* Do students get to examine how social status, hierarchy, respect, and power are exercised through communication practices, including praise, criticism, rumors, and gossip? Do students get suspended from school when they engage in poor judgment or do they get to reflect with their peers and their teachers on how their own communication behaviors shape the way they are treated by others?

Act: Make a Difference in the World

There's a relationship between education and citizenship—which is why media literacy education includes the concept of taking action. Educational theorists like Paulo Freire and John Dewey have shaped our thinking about how the classroom can be a place where students develop needed skills for engaging in genuine *ethical democratic citizenship.* Dewey asserted that learning cannot be standardized because it always takes place against the backdrop of the learner's particular knowledge and life experiences. For this reason, he suggested that teachers tie new material to their students' individual perspectives and give them the freedom to subject it to testing and debate.[14]

However, there are some scholars in the field of education who use the ideas of Paulo Freire and the concept of "empowerment" to refer to a highly abstracted and politicized form of cultural criticism that is disconnected from instructional practices of the classroom, the institutions of education, or the real-world practice of democracy. This is not what I mean by empowerment. Teachers whose form of social action is to "liberate" their students by helping them see the oppressive structures of capitalism and the superiority of a particular (leftist) critique may just be employing another type of propaganda instead of encouraging true dialogue that is necessary for civic action.

When students' ideas and thoughts move toward specific and concrete forms of social action, it can be energizing for young people and adults alike. When taking action is valued as a *communication competence* in Grades 7–12, students and teachers share knowledge and solve problems in the family, the workplace, and the community. Teachers create learning environments that are connected to local, regional, national, and international issues, helping students see a role for themselves as contributors to their own well-being and the lives of those around them.

- *Connect the classroom to the world.* Do classroom activities connect to relevant social issues, debates, and controversies in the world outside the classroom? Do students take action to address meaningful real-world problems that require solutions?
- *Support leadership and collaboration.* Do students get to use problem-solving skills to influence more than one person toward a goal? Do they recognize how to leverage the strengths of others to accomplish a common goal? Or do students just follow carefully described steps in a process already laid out by teachers?
- *Develop integrity and accountability.* Are students held accountable for their actions? Are situations and opportunities provided that enable students to discover how personal values like honesty and courtesy benefit the individual, the group, and the society?

Messages in a Wide Variety of Forms

Many teachers use a specially selected set of texts that are considered appropriate for the classroom. These might be textbooks, works of classic literature, or other materials that are easily recognizable as educational in nature. In some school districts, they may be selected by state school boards or vetted by a panel of experts. In some communities, questions about "what's appropriate" can become a political tug-of-war. In response, textbook publishers, testing agencies, professional associations, states, and the federal government have succumbed to pressure groups of left and right. That's because both right-wingers and left-wingers may "demand that publishers shield children from words and ideas that contain what they deem the 'wrong' models for living. Both assume that by limiting what children read, they can change society to reflect their worldview."[15]

Fortunately, in other schools and communities, teachers have great latitude to select resources and materials for use in the classroom. They don't need to use preselected books or get advance permission to show a video. In these communities, teachers are entrusted with professional responsibility to make wise choices.

Using a broad array of media texts and technology tools is an essential dimension of digital and media literacy education. It's a way of connecting the dots between the classroom and contemporary culture, helping students transfer skills between school and home. Consider how messages in a variety of forms are part of your curriculum by reviewing this list of different types of texts:

- *Daily Life.* These are the texts, tools, and technologies we encounter as part of ordinary life. We read brand names on our cereal boxes and our clothing. We may read an instruction manual online to install a cell phone app, look at a bus schedule, or fill out job application forms.

- *Academic.* These are the school-sanctioned texts in language arts, science, history, and math that introduce the subject matter to students or are used for learning purposes.

- *Professional.* These are the texts created by people in the world who work with ideas and information as part of their job. They might be a website, something from a professional magazine, or a research report.

- *Historical.* These are the texts of the past: newspaper articles from long ago, old-time radio dramas, historical artifacts from an archive, movies like *To Kill a Mockingbird,* and books from our parents' and grandparents' generation. Classic works of literature like *Romeo and Juliet* are also considered part of this category.

- *Mass Media and Popular Culture.* These are the texts that circulate as information and entertainment commodities. They are generally highly visible in contemporary culture. Articles from *The New York Times* or *Newsweek, Gossip Girl* episodes, scenes from movies like *Avatar,* video games, pop music, and other forms of entertainment and information are examples of these types of texts. Most forms of mass media are produced by companies as a means to sell audiences to advertisers.

- *Alternative Media.* These are texts created by organizations that don't see their work as a commodity designed to maximize profits. PBS is an example of alternative media, as are magazines like *In These Times* and TV shows like *Democracy Now.* Alternative media provide perspectives and ideas that aren't readily available in the profit-driven media world. There are alternative newspapers, magazines, television, radio, and film, as well as nontraditional media, such as zines, web-based publications, street theater, and murals.

- *Digital Culture.* There is no consensus yet about how to classify the many different types of digital content found on websites, blogs, wikis, and the many types of social media networks. Examples include collaboratively created sites like Wikipedia (www.wikipedia.org) as well as editorially vetted informational websites like Finding Dulcinea (www.findingdulcinea .com). Digital culture is vast—there are 10 billion photos on Facebook and 20 hours of video are uploaded to YouTube every minute.[16]

What this list reveals is the full range of authentic texts that people use as part of their social and cultural lives. All these forms can and should be used for teaching and learning—from kindergarten to college. Review the aforementioned list to consider how you make use of these various texts types in your own life—and in your classroom.

Research shows that using a wide variety of text types, including informational, historical, mass media, and alternative media texts, helps young people engage in more out-of-school reading and writing and create more linguistically complex texts.[17]

However, it takes practice to become comfortable using a wide range of informational texts in the classroom. Texts from mass media and popular culture may challenge and disrupt the routines of the classroom, shifting authority and power relationships between students and teachers. That's because when we use mass media and popular culture texts, students themselves have more knowledge and opinions to share. It's one of the *great debates* in media literacy: Should literacy educators include a focus on popular culture texts?[18] In this book, the answer is a resounding "yes," considering the obvious reason: Preparing students for life in contemporary society requires being knowledgeable about the role of media and technology in the daily lives of young people, activating all five digital and media literacy competencies, building bridges between the knowledge domains of school and home, and placing critical focus on the texts of popular culture, especially news, advertising, information, and entertainment.

CHAPTER 1 LESSON PLAN

Four Corners on the Media:
Reflecting on Our Love–Hate Relationship

Overview: Students participate in a conversation about the pleasures and troubling aspects of print, visual, sound, and digital media moving through the classroom in a "four-corners" activity. They then reflect on their own attitudes about these media by composing a reflective essay and share their writing with peers and the class.

Time: 1 class period plus homework

Resources Needed: Craft paper, colored markers

Learning Outcomes:

- Gain knowledge of the distinction between media texts and media types
- Recognize the value of personal experience as a form of knowing
- Strengthen listening and small group discussion skills
- Practice note taking as a way to organize and examine relationships between ideas
- Build awareness of discussion as a form of prewriting
- Strengthen public speaking and writing competencies

Preclass Preparation: Before class, put up sheets of craft paper in four corners of the room. Label each corner: PRINT, VISUAL, SOUND, and DIGITAL.

Introduction: Draw a picture of a heart and a devil's pitchfork on the board as you introduce the idea of a *love–hate relationship,* the idea that people can love something and hate some aspects of it at the same time. Preview the activity by explaining that students can reflect on their love–hate relationship with media and technology through small-group discussion to capture key ideas.

Explain Media Texts and Types: Explain that a text doesn't have to be written. A pop song is a text. So is a movie. *Texts* can be defined as symbolic expressions created by humans to share meaning. Then review the four types of media (print, visual, sound, and digital) by asking students to give specific examples of texts that fit into each category. Encourage students to be specific. Write their examples on the board. As they offer examples, you should note that the categories are blurry. For example, "audiobooks" could be placed into several of these categories.

Group Discussion: Break students into four groups and have each group move to one of the four corners of the room and discuss the positive and negative aspects of the one media form that's listed on the chart paper. Depending on the needs of your students, you may want to have students select a recorder to make notes or ask all students to contribute to making notes on the chart.

Rotate Groups: Every five minutes, move the groups to a different corner of the room and ask them to first review the notes made by the previous team, noting their agreement or disagreement with plusses and minuses. Then, encourage them to add more notes to the chart paper to add new ideas and offer nuance and depth to the ideas already on the chart paper.

Summarize: At the fifth rotation, students will arrive at their original corner of the room. Now they see that the chart they started has been transformed by other people's ideas. Ask students to read through the ideas and discuss the comments that were added. Have one or two students offer a summary of the most interesting ideas.

Homework: Explain that writing and thinking are related and as a result of sharing ideas with others, this activity has prepared students to express their unique point of view. Offer these choices to students:

> **Option 1.** Write a personal reflection of your own love–hate relationship with one of the four media forms, considering some of the key ideas that emerged from the classroom conversation.

> **Option 2.** Select one specific media text (like ABC's *Greek*, for example) and offer reflections on what you love and hate about it.

Expressive Options: If you prefer, students may complete this assignment as a blog entry or as a spoken word performance.

Read, Respond, and Share: Have students select a favorite sentence from their homework to read aloud. Then ask students to partner with a peer and read each other's work. Ask the partner to select a different favorite sentence and have that student read it aloud.

Whole Group Discussion: This writing assignment should stimulate more rich conversation about our love–hate relationship with media and technology. Encourage students to comment or offer a thought.

Summarize: Offer some reflections on your own love–hate relationship and point out how powerful it is to share and discuss the many paradoxes associated with the print, visual, sound, and digital texts that are part of our lives.

2

Research As
Authentic Inquiry

What You'll Find in This Chapter:

- While teaching the Arthur Miller play, *The Crucible,* a teacher uses students' knowledge about MTV reality shows to explore the relationship between drama, popular culture, and real life.
- Teachers don't need to be experts on youth media culture to open up important questions that link student experiences with media and technology to fundamental themes in the humanities.
- The practice of questioning assumptions about mass media through critical analysis supports the development of critical thinking and communication skills.
- Teaching the process of summarizing, paraphrasing, and direct quotation helps to solve the problem of cut-and-paste plagiarism.
- Using a process of generating authentic questions and gathering material for an evidence chart helps students to evaluate both high-quality information and poor-quality material.

Lesson Plan:

Create an Evidence Chart

I t was a bit of a crazy idea, Sam Fisher thought, as he drove into school that morning. But he knew he needed a fresh new way to make a connection with his Grade 10 students. He had considered starting the new year by reading Arthur Miller's play, *The Crucible,* a dramatization of the Salem witch trials. For years, he had done what many English teachers all over America do: read the book, then watch the movie. But he could see that the 1996 film wasn't capturing students' attention as it had in years past. Heads were down on many desks in the darkened classroom during the three or four periods needed for viewing. In his lower level classes, students were "SparkNoting" their way through the reading and then relying on the movie version for their understanding of the play.

All through the holiday break, Mr. Fisher had been feeling the need to deepen his connection to the life experiences of his students. In reflecting on what guiding question to use for exploring *The Crucible,* he felt that the topic of witchcraft had lost its appeal, the gender/power issues were old news to his students, and the Cold War angle was stale. How could he make the reading of *The Crucible* and the study of drama fresh and relevant to his students?

A teaching idea came to him when he stumbled by his teenage daughter's bedroom, where she was watching *16 and Pregnant,* the MTV reality show that traces the experiences of pregnant teenagers and their families. His daughter Gina was lying on her bed, using her computer to update her Facebook page while watching the show. What's it about? he asked, pointing to the TV screen. She launched into the backstory. In this episode, Catelynn is a high school junior from a small town in Michigan. Her mom is crazy. Her boyfriend, Tyler, has been her serious boyfriend since freshman year. Now Catelynn is pregnant, but neither she nor Tyler are ready to be parents. Their parents don't want them to put the baby up for adoption. Oh, and guess what? Catelynn's mom and Tyler's dad have fallen in love and have decided to get married. "This is one screwed up family," she explains to her dad, smiling. Gina likes this show. She and her dad had a good discussion about how the show cranks up the drama with its editing and use of suspense to keep you watching through the commercials.

After watching the rest of the episode with Gina, it was a compelling show, Sam Fisher discovered. Like *The Crucible,* it featured a teen girl getting a lot of negative attention from family and friends for her behavior. Viewers could identify with Catelynn as she wrestled with her guilt, self-interest, dependence, and sexual power. The dramatic tension between the parents and the teens echoed the themes of authority and dissent depicted within the world of *The Crucible.* At the end of the show, when Catelynn decides to put the baby up for adoption, despite her mom's strenuous objections, we're left wondering how this courageous decision will impact her relationship with her family and her reputation in her small, close-knit community. Mr. Fisher had to admit it—this MTV show addressed many of the themes of *The Crucible:* authority and dissent, martyrdom, community versus individual, accusation, guilt, love, redemption, and conscience.

When Mr. Fisher googled the show, he discovered that 3 million people watch this show. When he asked his daughter to find information about the show, within a couple of clicks, she had found a discussion board, with thousands of posts from teens all over the country. Reading through these posts, a new set of minidramas emerged, as teens, sometimes barely literate, typed out their questions, fears, and concerns. The *16 and Pregnant* website had become a place for young women all across the United States to share their anxieties about sexuality, about the experience of being pregnant, having babies, using protection (or not), or getting a sexually transmitted disease. Mr. Fisher was surprised to find a teacher discussion guide for each episode, offering information and questions for discussion. In it, there are questions such as these:

> Three out of ten girls in the United States will get pregnant at least once before age 20. One out of six girls will be a teenage mom. Have you ever thought about what your life would be like if you got pregnant or got someone pregnant?

> Did you know that only about 1% of teen girls who give birth choose adoption for their babies? Why do you think that is?

> If pregnant teens knew more about adoption, would they choose it more often? Is adoption too difficult a choice? Is it harder than becoming a parent too soon?

> Were you surprised by the fact that the baby's adoptive parents want Catelynn and Tyler to stay in contact with them and the baby? What do you think about that plan?[1]

The MTV show *16 and Pregnant* made drama out of the actual events of life experience, just as Arthur Miller did when he used the historical accounts of the Salem witch trials and turned them into a powerful narrative with compelling themes that reflected the concerns of his time. Mr. Fisher wondered if he could use this TV show to get his students thinking more deeply about the dramatic impulse: how playwrights apply imagination to the events of daily life, creating drama that derives its emotional power from its roots in reality.

In even considering the possibility of using this topic or this show in his classroom, Mr. Fisher had to face his own fears. Should he give the principal a heads-up before he started, letting him know that he'd be making a connection to a popular MTV show? He knew that the topic of teen sexuality was a battleground. He heard about the tension between comprehensive versus abstinence-only sexual education. Comprehensive sexual education communicates information about contraception and usually includes value-neutral discussion of abortion, sexual orientation, and other controversial topics. Abstinence-only curricula is the "just say no" approach to sex education, promoting abstinence as the only acceptable standard for youth—and indeed for anyone not in a heterosexual marriage. Abstinence-only curricula do not mention contraception, except to emphasize failure rates.[2] Fortunately, in his school, the health program offered a comprehensive approach to sex education.

Mr. Fisher also recognized that this topic would open up issues about sexuality, the body, and identity in ways that could challenge or reinscribe gender stereotypes. He was aware of how much students' understanding of feminism is shaped through the media, from the Dove "Real Beauty" campaign to the image of a pregnant Britney Spears on the cover of *Harper's Bazaar,* to Pink's "Stupid Girls" song, where she sings about young women who seek to live up to the beauty standards and consumer habits set by Hollywood stars (in her video she imitates Lindsey Lohan, Paris Hilton, and Jessica Simpson). In an interview with Oprah, Pink explained that she wrote the song to spark discussion about "mindless consumerism," about women not "questioning anything or contributing anything to the world."[3] The paradoxes at work in exploring this issue are evident as adolescents recognize that Pink exploits her own body and her own sexuality even while criticizing others who do the same.

He knew he would have to be attentive to create a climate where students were sensitive to how their words would be interpreted by others. He would have to make sure that the class didn't descend into the kind of "girls vs. boys" stupidity that students sometimes enjoy. However this lesson developed, Mr. Fisher knew from long experience that it could provide rich opportunities to explore how the "complex social dynamics of difference and inequality" are represented in contemporary culture and the issue of "making a space where the media's version of the 'norm' can be questioned."[4]

Honoring What Students Know

Children and young people grow up in mediaspheres that adults can find difficult to understand. Similarly, many young people find the preoccupations of the adult world to be remote, disconnected from their lives, and incomprehensible.

This fragmentation of culture is evident across all aspects of contemporary life, in news and current events, politics, and the arts. Young people are growing up in multicultural societies where, as David Buckingham has explained, "very different conceptions of morality and very different cultural traditions exist side-by-side."[5] As much as some educators might like to think of themselves as transmitters of the official culture, we now must help students become active, critical interpreters of contemporary culture, helping them grasp the multiple realities and diverse forms of knowledge and experience that are circulating in this dense and ever-changing stew. For this reason, media literacy education has long been understood as a mechanism to reduce the gap between the world of the classroom and the living room.[6]

Because Mr. Fisher was an experienced teacher, he knew that he could have an authentic conversation with students about teen pregnancy and the representation of gender, power, and sexuality on popular TV channels like MTV. He knew he could help students appreciate the similarities between the fear, suspicion, social ostracism, and emotional upheavals of teen pregnancy and the vengeful accusations of witchcraft in 17th-century Salem.

As the father of a teenage girl, he knew that his students were active in their consumption of reality TV dramas. But he wasn't quite sure what would happen when exploring the whole genre of dramatic teenage reality shows on MTV. Should he show an episode of *16 and Pregnant* in the classroom? Should he attempt a Venn diagram comparison–contrast project with *The Crucible*?

The place to start was by figuring out what students knew and thought about reality TV teen shows like *16 and Pregnant*. For Mr. Fisher, MTV was an alien planet network ever since it stopped airing music videos many years ago. But he knew how to activate students' prior knowledge in ways that deepen their reflective thinking about language. Giving students a handout with the names of MTV reality shows listed, he asked them to write a description of as many shows as they could, putting each description on one of the largest size of lined sticky notes.

> ## Describing MTV Shows
>
> Activity: Write one or two well-formed sentences to describe each of the shows listed below. Put each show name and description on a single sticky note.
>
> | | | |
> |---|---|---|
> | *Pranked* | *If You Really Knew Me* | *Moving In* |
> | *16 and Pregnant* | *The Real World:* | *True Life* |
> | *The Hills* | *Washington D.C.* | *Nitro Circus* |
> | *Silent Library* | *The Buried Life* | *Teen Mom* |
> | *Jersey Shore* | *My Life As Liz* | *World of Jenks* |
> | *Taking the Stage* | *Teen Cribs* | *Fantasy Factory* |
> | *Bully Beatdown* | *The City* | *Parental Control* |

One morning in January, he tried the assignment and it worked: As students wrote their descriptions, the room was so quiet and so intense that Mr. Fisher was astonished. When he then asked students to pair up and discuss the similarities and differences between their descriptions, the hubbub in the room was palpable. Students immediately started talking to each other and the energy in the room was intense. As he walked around the room, he heard a lot of different opinions. It was clear that students were really listening to each other. Not all students were familiar with *all* these shows, but every student seemed to have something to say, even those who had only seen the promotional commercials.

Then he passed out more sticky notes and asked students to collaboratively revise their sentences by incorporating the best elements from both partners. There was substantial effort made in writing the descriptive sentences, as students edited, crossed out, crumpled up notes, and revised their descriptions while engaged in lively discussion with their partner. In fact, the discussions were so intense and authentic that Mr. Fisher let students talk and write the whole period, collecting the large sticky notes as they left. "Wow, that was fun, Mr. Fisher," one student said as she headed out the room. He knew that he could up the ante now, explaining that since his students were now fully engaged, he could "kick it up a notch," as the saying goes.

Teaching Contemporary Drama

The connection between media literacy and the fine and performing arts is rich. Through exploring drama and theater arts, students develop interpersonal skills and problem-solving capabilities through group interaction; they apply the creative process to fundamental skills of acting, playwriting, and directing; they relate the role of theater arts to culture and history, analyzing the characteristics of traditional and modern forms of dramatic expression. Connecting the worlds of school, media, and home through the theme of drama was Mr. Fisher's challenge here.

Defining Drama

Drama is the specific mode of fiction represented in performance. The term comes from a Greek word meaning *action*. The enactment of drama in theater, performed by actors on a stage before an audience, involves collaborative modes of production and a collective form of reception.

The next day, Mr. Fisher had written the definition of drama on the board and posted students' large sticky notes, show by show, all over the room. First, they unpacked the definition to discuss concepts like "performance," "enactment," "collaborative," and "collective." He then invited students to compare and contrast how different groups had described these shows. He invited them to consider whether the MTV shows listed on the board deserved to be called dramas, based on the definition provided. After students did a *gallery walk* around the room, he asked pairs of students to stand next to where a group of sticky notes were displayed and, after reviewing the descriptions, summarize the similarities and differences they noticed.

Discussion was lively. Students had opinions about the variety of sentences that their peers had written on their sticky notes. And the minipresentations on each TV show that students delivered were eye-opening. Was *My Life as Liz* a reality show about a high school girl who's a little geeky and weird or was it a scripted drama that just looked like a reality show? Are the boys in *The Buried Life* an inspiring group of young people trying to find meaning in life, or are they just goofing off in front of the camera? Should *Nitro Circus,* featuring young adults engaging in bizarre and often humiliating stunts, be described as disgusting or entertaining? Each minipresentation resulted in a round of playful, open, and thoughtful comments, punctuated by occasionally nuanced discussion as students wanted to ask questions, dispute, add, or clarify points.

Mr. Fisher noticed that students were actually engaged in talking about language. It mattered to them *what words were used* to describe these shows. And it was evident that there were different levels of knowledge in the classroom about these programs. Students were enjoying sharing their expertise and their opinions. Some offered up minitreatises on the show, with critical commentary, while other reports were more tentative and sketchy. It was loud in the room at times. The dynamic quality of the conversation revealed that students were having fun! They were sharing ideas and listening to others.

Without any prompting from Mr. Fisher, students themselves started to spontaneously debate about the different ways that the word "drama" is used in contemporary discourse: It could mean a type of movie or TV show, but it could also mean a type of action. It also could mean a particular set of behaviors or even a feeling, a sensibility, a tone. These meanings are different than the definition of drama presented on the board, Mr. Fisher noted, since words have *meaning in context,* and through usage, meaning changes.

Reality TV is just a new type of drama, blurring fact and fiction in ways that keep audiences psychologically involved in the lives and experiences of the characters. In reality TV shows, the realism of the relationships and the emotions combines with the sensational and melodramatic to create a powerful emotional brew. When the classic plotlines of narrative storytelling, the unpredictability of reality, and the sheer thrill of melodrama are combined, the psychological effects can be powerful.

For young people today, reality TV has always been part of their lives since the first episode of *Big Brother* aired on CBS in 2000. Returning to *The Crucible,* students in Mr. Fisher's class began to see how Arthur Miller's dramatization of American history was similar to the dramatization of daily life that we see on reality TV shows. Students were more curious than in years past, it seemed to Mr. Fisher, about the real story of the Salem witch trials, since the theme of "blurred distinctions between reality and make-believe" had been foregrounded for students. They asked questions about the controversy of the mid-20th century, when the House Un-American Activities Committee and Senator Joseph McCarthy were engaged in another type of witch hunt in seeking out Communists in entertainment media.

By letting students bring in their own rich media experiences with the blurring of drama and life, their English teacher had made a connection that had relevance and meaning for them, helping them engage with a classic work of American drama, examine the psychological and social functions of drama, and reflect on their own viewing pleasures at home.

Opening Up or Closing Down Discourse

Mr. Fisher knew that he was no expert on the topic of teen reality TV shows. He didn't know where the inquiry process would lead. But he had successfully created a structure in the classroom that got kids to start talking. And because he was the father of a teenage daughter, he had plenty of his own opinions about the genre. Every once in a while, he wanted to give students his own opinions, telling them what to think about these shows. As Donna Alvermann and her colleagues explain, "At times, adults position themselves as more knowledgeable about the meanings adolescents make of popular culture, and assume they already know what those meanings will be. When this happens, adults stabilize the meaning of the text, according to their own perceptions and experiences of it, foreclosing other possible meanings of and uses for texts that adolescents might create on their own."[7]

A similar attitude is just as problematic when adults position themselves as distanced from or critical of the mass media, popular culture, and digital media that students enjoy. However, Alvermann and her colleagues point out that youth are ready and willing to talk with adults about popular culture if adults show a willingness to learn. They explain, "Instead of traveling into what we perceive as youth territory to learn from as well as to teach, adults habitually stay safely distanced from these areas, thinking that youth's popular culture is of little interest to their adult tastes or that youth would not want to share these interests with adults."[8] Of course, teachers don't need to display either their expertise or their lack of knowledge when popular culture texts are being interrogated. Listening and asking questions are the most important practices that activate critical thinking in the high school classroom.

Generating Authentic Questions

In the process of opening up the relationship between reality TV and drama, Mr. Fisher's students spontaneously generated a number of authentic questions arising from this activity, including the following:

- Why are there so many reality shows?
- How do you get hired to be on a reality show?
- How are reality shows made?

- What is a "scripted" reality show?
- Are men or women the target audience for reality shows?
- Do people identify with or laugh at the characters on reality shows?
- Do the creators of reality TV shows think of themselves as playwrights or producers?
- What happens to people on reality shows after the show is over?
- What other famous plays have been based on true stories?
- What is the difference between melodrama and drama?
- How accurate is *The Crucible?* Where did Arthur Miller get his information?
- Can you get into legal trouble by making a fictional drama out of a true story?
- Was *The Crucible* considered a controversial play when it was first produced?
- Was the playwright Arthur Miller a controversial person during his lifetime?
- What other plays did he write?

The list was just so good. These were some fascinating topics. And even the most reluctant underachievers had contributed something to the list. Mr. Fisher knew he would have to move his research paper assignment up from April, where he usually did it at the end of the year because he wasn't really that interested in teaching about database searching or the mechanics of MLA citation. Plus, when one of the technology teachers showed him the 123 Help Me website (www.123helpme.com), with over 600 mostly repetitive and boring student-written essays on the play, all with rehashing of plot and themes, and all available for a small fee, Mr. Fisher knew that he probably had students who used this service or something similar in the past. He knew he needed a fresh approach. What if Mr. Fisher modeled the practice of gathering information for a research paper, using this inquiry as a place to start?

Today, many teachers across the curriculum are developing creative strategies to make teaching the research paper more relevant. One teacher asked a team of students to gather research information to script a special episode of *Oprah* featuring historical figures from the French revolution. Another teacher designed an assignment where students were to choose a piece of popular culture that would still be important 10 years from now and explain why it was still popular. Students were encouraged to use reviews of television shows, movies, music, and a wide range of online source materials to develop the topic.[9]

Media Literacy and the Practice of Questioning Assumptions: A History

With user-created encyclopedias, university-sponsored websites, bloggers, news aggregators, and other new forms of content online, there's easy access to a wide range of information, assertions, gossip, rumors, and opinions. Not only is it important to be able to identify the source of information, we must also examine the quality of information we encounter. Fortunately, the practice of questioning content and exploring unstated assumptions has been part of the 20th-century tradition in English education. For example, back in the 1930s, when asked what's needed for being a good writer, Ernest Hemingway replied, "crap detecting skills." The foundational idea that English education supports the development of critical thinking skills is rooted in this robust tradition.

During the 1960s, new approaches to English education were developing as a result of rapid and dramatic changes in culture and technology brought about by the cultural rise of television. Neil Postman explained how English teachers could help students develop a built-in crap detector at a presentation to the 1969 National Council of Teachers of English conference in Washington, D.C. He said, "As I see it, the best things schools can do for kids is to help them learn how to distinguish useful talk from bullshit. . . . Every day in almost every way people are exposed to more bullshit than it is healthy for them to endure."[10]

Neil Postman was proposing an approach to English education that has at its center not "covering" works of classic literature but instead sharpening focus on the practice of critical thinking, the practice of questioning assumptions. Postman wanted English education to help people live better lives, not just recruit kids to major in English in college. He wondered how education would change if educators really made use of the dominant technologies of the time. Back in 1970, he described *multimedia literacy* as including texts of popular culture, including music, movies, television, and comics, as well as student media production, with kids using 8mm films, photography, and graphic design alongside language and the printed word.

In an essay published in the *Harvard Educational Review,* Postman wished that this new multimedia literacy would reshape conceptualizations of what counts as intelligence. He wrote, "At present, the only way those on the top can maintain control is by carefully discriminating against what the students know—that is, by labeling what the students know as unimportant." If students could use media as a rich source of content to explore and as a medium of self-expression, Postman explained, the old hierarchies based on unequal access to information would crumble and students and "schools would be a place where everybody, including the adults, is trying to learn something. Such a school would obviously be problem-centered and future-centered and change-centered, and as such, would be an instrument of cultural and political radicalism. In the process we might find that our youth would also learn to read without pain and with a degree of success and economy not presently known."[11]

For over four decades now, many educators have since followed in Postman's epistemological footsteps, eschewing an exclusive focus on lecturing on the causes of the Civil War or reading particular works of classic or contemporary literature. Instead, time is spent to "begin with youth and community concerns," using knowledge and practice "as a way of making the learning of disciplinary knowledge more accessible to youth."[12]

Research evidence shows the power of student talk as a stimulus that supports both reading and writing competencies. We also know from test score results across the United States that simply reading six, eight, or twelve works of classic literature in a year doesn't meet most of our students' real needs when it comes to developing reading and writing skills. One researcher looked at how expert teachers model historical reasoning and found that student writing improves when teachers make many opportunities for students to take over much of the oral discourse of the classroom, providing scaffolded opportunities to practice historical reasoning, which includes using narrative, hypothesis generation, and critical assessment, and the ability to contextualize claims. Oral explaining—with both students and teachers participating—develops reasoning skills that support reading and writing practices across the disciplines.[13]

Authentic Inquiry:
Modeling the Research Process

After generating research questions, Mr. Fisher asked students to write lists of search terms when the class went to the library for some preliminary research. Mr. Fisher discovered that some students were not able to generate a robust list of keywords. Some kids typed the whole question into the Google search bar. Depending on the question, sometimes this worked to produce results, but other times it was ineffective. To capitalize on this teachable moment, Mr. Fisher illustrated the difference in results by typing in "What kinds of jobs do people on reality shows get after the show is over?" and comparing the results to those found using the keywords "reality TV, post-show, characters, actors." Students were attentive and active during this lesson because they were interested in both the content and the process used to gather information.

School librarians tell us that, when looking for information online, many young people give up before they find what they need. People often use a small number of search strategies in a repetitive way even when they do not get the information they are seeking. They don't take the time to digest and evaluate what they encounter. In many cases, "students typically use information that finds them, rather than deciding what information *they* need."[14]

When researchers look at how people acquire information and how this has changed over time, it is obvious that people value quick, instant access to information. The way we read online illustrates this. One researcher notes, "Power browsing—skimming online pages and clicking on hyperlinks—displaces traditional sequential reading and longer term creative and critical thinking. Little use is made of advanced search facilities, and many display difficulty in judging the relevance of online information or indeed the authority of the online sources."[15] By the way, this behavior is common among all users, from older people to those who have grown up with new technologies.

After Mr. Fisher watched how random and inefficient students' search strategies were, he decided to systematically model his own search strategies, displaying the process on the data projector while talking aloud to make his reasoning and thinking processes explicit.

Within minutes, his keyword search strategy yielded a surprising essay by radio talk show host Tim Mihalsky from the *Huffington Post*, who interviewed Kristin Cavallari, star of MTV's *The Hills*, who commented that her own reputed drug use was just a public relations effort designed to get ratings. One blogger wrote about the questionable ethics involved: "How far would you go—at the risk of damaging your reputation with your real friends and family—to get ratings for a TV show? I think faking or even hinting at a drug problem goes too far."[16] In-classroom exploration of this website made his students alert, engaged, and expectant. Why? Such moral and ethical questions are truly meaningful to young people who are learning to balance their natural idealism with a deeper understanding of social and institutional power as well as the complexities of human nature.

> **A Sample of State Standards for the Research Process in English Language Arts, Grades 9–12**
>
> - Formulate research questions
> - Determine how to locate necessary information
> - Examine critical relationships between and among elements of the research topic
> - Use systematic strategies to record and organize information
> - Achieve balance between research information and original ideas
> - Synthesize information into a logical sequence
> - Paraphrase information and integrate direct quotation into the flow of the paper
> - Use bibliography to document reference sources[17]

A Solution to Cut-and-Paste Plagiarism

With the tremendous volume of knowledge now available to us at the touch of a finger, the teaching of research strategies is more important than ever before across all disciplines and subject areas. While some students receive systematic instruction in research strategies in the elementary grades, many others learn and practice a variety of informal cut-and-paste strategies for some years before they arrive in high school. It's important to understand student attitudes about plagiarism. A survey of high school students found that about 35% of students had directly copied and pasted material into an assignment without citation, and of these students, only half had considered it plagiarism or cheating.[18] As explanation, students offer these reasons:

Lack of Confidence. "I'm not good at writing papers."

Ease. "It's easier and faster if I copy."

Necessity. "I need this information for my paper."

Peer Pressure. "I know that my friends do it."

Paraphrasing. "I copy and paste but then change around the information."

Research has shown that teachers' own attitudes about plagiarism have a significant impact on their students. When teachers are confused about what constitutes plagiarism, they may inadvertently pass along problematic practices to their students. One study found that 17% of students were actively being encouraged by their teachers to copy,[19] perhaps because of lack of clarity in introducing the skills of summarizing, paraphrasing, and direct quotation.

Students learn effective strategies for building new ideas using the works of others when they get opportunities to practice these skills:

Summarizing involves finding the thesis statement or topic sentence and condensing the major ideas into a brief passage. Summarizing is the most challenging of the three skills for managing information in the research process.

Paraphrasing is sometimes defined as "putting the content of a message into one's own words." It's actually much easier than summarizing because it's essentially an act of translation. In explaining why paraphrasing supports the reading process, Sharon Kletzien wrote, "Paraphrasing encourages the reader to make connections with prior knowledge to access what is already known about the topic and to use words that are already part of the reader's knowledge," helping the reader integrate what is previously known with what is being read.[20]

Direct quotation is an art, since it demands that the writer not only select a powerful phrase but connect it purposefully to the writer's own ideas. Direct quotes can be used to build credibility, convey the unique style or voice of a source, or capture key facts. Even at the college level, students often need considerable practice in effectively integrating direct quotations into their writing.

Building an Evidence Chart to Explore the Quality of Information

To encourage students to gather information while being self-conscious about their decisions about what counts as credible knowledge, Mr. Fisher asked students to work with a partner to explore one or more of the questions the class had created. Their assignment: Create an evidence chart with a range of sources, arranged from "excellent" in quality to "awful" in quality. The lesson plan at the end of the chapter shows this assignment in detail. Students were encouraged to search not only for high-quality information but also for information that was less trustworthy and believable.

What Is an Evidence Chart?

A poster or other visual display that organizes 10 different information sources in vertical order, from *most* credible to *least* credible. For each information source, students do the following:

1. Summarize, paraphrase, or select a direct quotation of a key piece of information from the source

2. Compose a correctly formatted citation

3. Offer an explanation of why it should be ranked more or less credible

To find 10 sources of information of varying quality, this assignment demanded that students find examples of content that is often considered not legitimate for academic work. For example, students found personal home pages that are maintained by individual fans and former reality TV show contestants. They found special interest sites that are maintained by activists or nonprofit organizations. They found professional sites that report on the television industry, as well as news and journalistic sites that included more and less reputable forms of celebrity and industry journalism. And they found commercial sites, including material from public relations firms, agents, photographers, acting coaches, and lawyers. Figure 2.1 shows an example of this assignment.

Because the research questions were authentic and meaningful to them, students had fun with this project. The assignment gave students permission to examine informational resources that are not generally considered appropriate for school. By breaking down epistemological hierarchies of knowledge, students enjoy the opportunity to play with previously marginalized sources of information. This assignment allowed everyone (teacher and students alike) to discover that expertise is not exclusively found in peer-reviewed articles found in library databases. Plenty of high-quality information is available on blogs, commercial websites, and other sources sometimes ignored when teachers focus exclusively on academic writing found in library databases.

"It was harder than I thought to find bad information," said one student after completing this assignment. "I really had to dig around online for it. And it was sometimes difficult to actually explain why we thought the quality was good or poor—maybe it was the way the

Figure 2.1   Creating an Evidence Chart

CITATION: Caramanica, J. (2010). At 40, Circling Back to Teenage Life. New York Times, August 27.

SUMMARY: The producer of *16 and Pregnant* has had a turbulent career after having a successful early start in Hollywood followed by a string of failures and personal problems. Now that *16 and Pregnant* is a hit, he has a mission to tell the complex life stories of teenagers who are struggling with life challenges (Caramanica, 2010).

PARAPHRASE: More than 2.4 million viewers watch *16 and Pregnant* each week (Caramanica, 2010).

DIRECT QUOTATION: Morgan J. Freeman has helped "reposition MTV's reality slate from tracking the lives of the young, beautiful and rich to capturing the lives of the young, beautiful and resilient" (Caramanica, 2010, p. D1).

EVALUATION: This article is an interview with the executive producer of *16 and Pregnant*, but because it's a personal story about his career, it's not the highest quality source for my project, even though it is from the *New York Times*, which is a newspaper with a good reputation.

site looked, or what kinds of hyperlinks were used." But the student then explained that it was a fun assignment—and she ended up getting access to some really fascinating information, too. When the evidence charts were posted in class, students eagerly read the work of other students. They had enjoyed the chance to criticize poor-quality or questionable information sources. Most importantly, the evidence charts offered answers to research questions that they had generated themselves as part of a process of authentic inquiry.

Digging Deeper: What Counts as Knowledge

When it comes to online information, few of us verify the information we find online. *Verification* involves finding multiple sources, identifying the author or purpose, or examining the quality of evidence used. It's not an easy process, by any means. Both adults and young people tend to uncritically trust information we find, from whatever source. With so many sources of information available, assessing credibility is difficult. That's because with no editorial gatekeeper, the content available on the Internet often blurs the lines between amateur and professional, entertainment and marketing, and information and persuasion.

Some websites lack the necessary information we need to evaluate message quality. We may experience a *context deficit*, where not knowing enough about the author, purpose, and target audience of a website impairs our judgment. In some cases, information about authorship is unavailable, masked, or entirely missing. For example, websites that aggregate information may display materials from multiple sources on one webpage, which may itself be inaccurately perceived as the source. Hyperlinking may make it even more difficult for users to follow and evaluate multiple sources[21] as we move with the touch of a mouse click to access information presented by multiple authors, each with a different agenda and point of view.

People often use superficial criteria for assessing the quality of information. These are mental shortcuts (called *heuristics*) that generally serve a good purpose. Heuristics speed information processing and we use them automatically. The most common one is aligned with the idea that "If it looks good, it is good." That's why cues like graphic design help us to evaluate the credibility of a source. It is no different when it comes to people as sources of information, by the way. When we get information from others, we consider factors like likeability and attractiveness, which affect our decisions about the credibility of people, information, and ideas.

Another heuristic is based on the truism, "If others think it is good, it is good." That's because family, co-workers, and friends influence our decisions about who and what to trust. Today, judgments about what's credible can also be shaped by participation in online communities. We assess quality, credibility, and reliability by considering social characteristics of network environments. A person who has 5,000 Twitter followers is someone we assume is more credible than one with 12 followers. When Amazon or Netflix ratings show that a book or movie is highly rated, this is another type of social cue that serves as an aid to making decisions.[22] When a YouTube video is seen by millions of viewers, it's because an *informational cascade* has led to rapid sharing, because much of people's everyday behavior is shaped by their understanding of what others think and do.[23]

Both the immediacy and immersive social characteristics of digital media are a double-edged sword. Who doesn't love the ease of surfing and searching? It's one of the greatest social benefits of the Internet. But because it is so easy, we may be discouraged from reflective, analytic thinking about sources, content, and credibility. It's just so simple—point, click, and wow, you're on to something new.

That's why people who pay attention to the quality of media messages tend to have a general understanding of human perceptual and cognitive processes. Among these include our natural tendencies to value sources as credible only when they reinforce our existing beliefs and attitudes. People trust the sources that *match our existing opinions* and we distrust information that challenges our beliefs. Awareness of this tendency can help people become more open and receptive to diverse sources and points of view. People also need increased awareness of the practice of *source monitoring*, the process of making judgments about the origin of information. Unless we are vigilant, we tend to detach information content from its source, forgetting where it came from.[24] Increased knowledge of human information processing and personal awareness and self-reflection can help address these challenges.

Putting It All Together

After students' evidence charts had been posted, Mr. Fisher asked them to review the evidence charts around the room. With 14 evidence charts created by the student partner teams, each consisting of 10 sources, students had a lot of stuff hanging on the wall. With these resources at their disposal, each student was responsible for creating an outline of a short five-paragraph research paper, with a thesis statement, development of key ideas, conclusion, and reference list.

Before letting students go around the room to harvest the best ideas, he first demonstrated an approach to organize and sequence information found from source materials. Mr. Fisher modeled the process by using PowerPoint, in a lesson plan idea he borrowed from Michael Eisenberg, a professor specializing in information literacy whose work he had seen at a professional conference. Standing in front of one of the evidence charts after class, he typed in the information he wanted to use on the slide and the full citation in the notes section of the same slide. When showing his work to students, he used the Slide Sorter function to organize the information, moving the slides around until he was happy with the sequence. Then he downloaded the slides into a Word document. Then students used this technique to develop their own print outlines.

"Not only did we really get to think deeply about the nature of drama as it attempts to represent the complexity of human relationships, but I think students also got a better understanding of research as a truly creative process," he explained at the end of the semester.

CHAPTER 2 LESSON PLAN

Create an Evidence Chart

Now that you have developed your research question, it's time to find some information to answer it. An evidence chart is a poster or other visual display that organizes 10 different information sources in vertical order, from "most credible" to "least credible." Using library and online sources, your job is to find "the good, the bad, and the ugly." You'll be on the lookout for 4 sources that are "outstanding," 3 sources that are "average," and 3 that are truly "mediocre," but all 10 sources must address your research question in some way.

For each information source you select, (1) summarize, paraphrase, or select a direct quotation of a key piece of information from the source, (2) compose a correctly formatted citation, and (3) offer an explanation of why it ranks as more or less credible.

Here's a suggested way to organize your work:

1. **Keep Your Goal in Mind.** Write out your research question. Your purpose is to find information to answer your research question by reviewing a collection of both higher and lower quality sources.

2. **Cite Your Sources.** As you find a source, write the complete citation. For this assignment, you should also make a screen shot of the page so that you can use that in your poster. You can use EasyBib or a similar online tool for formatting citations and keeping track of your materials.

3. **Evaluate.** Is it a higher quality source or a lower quality source? This assessment will depend on both your purpose and the characteristics of the source.

4. **Read and Write.** Read the content of your source material carefully. As you read, consider how the content relates to your purpose and goal. Compose a summary, a paraphrase, and a direct quotation using (author, date) internal citation for each one.

5. **Create Your Posters.** Using the visual example, create 10 PowerPoint slides. Each slide should contain a visual that represents your source; a full citation, a summary, paraphrase, and direct quotation; and a description of your evaluation of the quality.

6. **Arrange Slides in Vertical Order From Most to Least Credible.** Be prepared to explain your reasoning about the order you choose.

Three Ways to Use Source Materials

Paraphrasing is a type of translation where you put specific informative details of the message content into your own words.

Summarizing involves finding the overall main idea of the content and condensing the major ideas into a brief passage.

Direct quotation is selecting a powerful phrase that can be connected purposefully to your own ideas. Direct quotes can be used to build credibility, convey the unique style or voice of a source, or capture key facts

Evaluating the Credibility of Source Materials

Author: Who created this message? Is this a well-known source? What is the source's reputation?

Quality of Content: What is the focus of the information? How useful is it? Is the information verified? Is it consistent with other high-quality sources?

Tone and Purpose: What's the motive for why it's been created? Is the purpose to inform, to persuade, or to entertain? Does the tone of the writing seem professional or biased?

Design: Is the message well-organized? Attractive? Readable?

ANALYZE

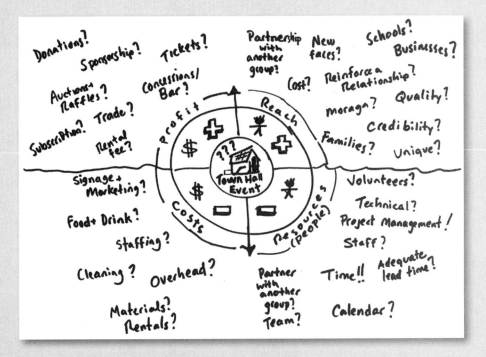

3

Critical Questions, Close Reading

What You'll Find in This Chapter:

- Blogging about current events strengthens students' critical analysis and communication skills and promotes intellectual curiosity about history and literature in ways that are aligned with Common Core State Standards.
- Seven instructional practices help educators use the ever-changing texts of mass media, popular culture, and digital media in ways that support academic achievement.
- The media literacy remote control is a visual metaphor that helps students engage in close analysis of text.
- Critical questions about authors, audiences, messages, meanings, representations, and realities encourage active interpretation and reasoning, using textual evidence to support one's ideas.
- When middle-school students express their ideas about what makes books, movies, TV shows, and video games seem realistic or unrealistic, they gain confidence and strengthen communication skills by developing a position and defending a point of view in a formal oral presentation.

Lesson Plan:

Five Critical Questions

Spiro Bolos and John O'Connor coteach an American studies course at New Trier High School in suburban Chicago. It's a course that's been part of the high school's curriculum since the 1960s, when faculty teaching English and history used common themes to maintain a sense of integration during the school year. The course is an inquiry-based study of American narratives through the use of artifacts (novels, short stories, poems, nonfiction works, films, visual arts, and primary source documents). It combines rhetoric, analysis, and reflection to integrate the English and social studies disciplines. It tackles three thematic paradoxes of American culture: individualism and community, idealism and pragmatism, and diversity and unity.

Cross-disciplinary integration can take many forms. In some schools, students take American literature during the same year they take American history. In other schools, students read works from 19th-century literature concurrently while studying this historical period. But at New Trier High School, American studies is team-taught by English and social studies teachers as one course. Teachers work together for the whole year. Throughout the whole process, Mr. Bolos and Mr. O'Connor plan, coteach, and evaluate student work together. So do the eight other teachers who offer this course at New Trier. To make it work, each course enrolls 40–50 students for an 85-minute period. As teachers explain, "The course privileges depth more than breadth. The inquiry-based nature of the course demands that questions, not coverage, be the focus."[1]

In the fall of 2010, for the first week of class, students tackled a discussion of the building of "the mosque at Ground Zero" by listening to a National Public Radio (NPR) story about the controversy. The story commented on how the phrase used to describe the mosque contains inaccurate and misleading information. The site of the proposed Islamic center is actually in the former Burlington Coat Factory building, located two blocks away from the former World Trade Center in a busy commercial area. That's why the Associated Press (AP) sent out a memo to its staff discouraging use of the phrase, explaining, "We should continue to avoid the phrase 'ground zero mosque' or 'mosque at ground zero.'"

At the class website (www.anamericanstudies.com), students reflected on a writing prompt. Through blogging, they were encouraged to analyze the coverage of the AP's decision to communicate to its staff, using the five critical questions of media literacy. During the year, students then learned more about the first time the phrase "ground zero" was used to refer to the nuclear bombing of Hiroshima and Nagasaki.

This assignment opened the school year with a bang by using a highly emotional current events issue to encourage students to reflect on the power of language to shape social and political reality. Within a few days, students had contributed ideas online. Mr. Bolos wrote responses to student writing—acknowledging the best ideas, suggesting ways to improve the writing, and provoking more questions.

Regular frequent writing that encourages students to demonstrate their analysis skills is an effective approach to learning. In reflecting on her growth over the course of the year, one New Trier High School student wrote this: "I think my blogging experience has allowed me to grow as a student this year. Before this blog, when I found an interesting article or topic, I didn't know how to share this interest with others. This blog has given me an outlet to express opinions about topics I wouldn't otherwise be able to share with others. And on top of that, I am actively able to use the skills I learned this year. To be honest, before this year, I didn't think as critically about articles and books, but blogging and commenting on others' blogs has allowed me to put this skill to use while engaging with my peers and using their ideas to further my own posts. I also like the informal nature of blogging and the ability to interact with my classmates through topics I find interesting."[2] Through blogging, students discover their voices in ways that support academic achievement.

Common Core Standards

Digital and media literacy education is well-aligned with Common Core State Standards. When the National Governors Association Center for Best Practices and the Council of Chief State School Officers (CCSSO) released a set of state-led education standards, there was a mixture of both relief and confusion. Differences between state standards and state tests had created a nightmare for assessing the quality of education across states. The Common Core State Standards for Grades K–12 were developed in collaboration with a variety of stakeholders including content experts, states, teachers, school administrators, and parents. The activities and ideas presented in this book are consistent with these Common Core State Standards. Goals for students include:

- **Students demonstrate independence**. By asking relevant questions and building on others' ideas, they seek out and use resources to become self-directed learners.
- **Students comprehend as well as critique.** Students read purposefully and refine and share their knowledge. They question an author or speaker's assumptions and assess the veracity of

claims and soundness of reasoning. They use evidence when supporting their ideas and make their reasoning clear. Students adapt their communication in relation to audience, task, purpose, and discipline.

- **Students use technology and digital media strategically and capably.** They are familiar with the strengths and limitations of various technological tools and media and select and use those best suited for their communication goals.

Instructional Practices of Digital and Media Literacy Education

There are seven instructional practices that help educators use the ever-changing texts of mass media, popular culture, and digital media in ways that support academic achievement. In order to connect the classroom to the culture, teachers should make active use of what is currently happening in everyday life—and that changes fast. Because digital media, mass media, and popular culture are so dynamic, it's not always practical to rely on preproduced curriculum materials. Some of the best lessons will come from using current events, websites, movie clips, TV shows, video games, or music that you learn about from your students, read about in the newspaper, or hear about on the radio.

That's why these seven instructional practices of media literacy education have so much value. These activities can be used with any set of media texts, tools, or technologies. That is why digital and media literacy education can be easily integrated into a variety of subjects. Here are seven core instructional techniques:

- **Media diary** (keeping reflective records of media consumption habits)
- **Search strategies** (learning to ask questions, find and evaluate information from a variety of sources)
- **Reading, viewing, listening, and discussion** (comprehending a message and sharing interpretations)
- **Close analysis of texts** (using critical questioning and Socratic dialogue)
- **Multimedia composition** (creating a media message for a particular audience and an authentic purpose)
- **Cross-media comparison** (analyzing two different media messages that address the same topic)
- **Simulation and role playing** (exploring points of view and the decision-making process)

These instructional practices help teachers to create a well-ordered, active, and respectful learning environment where learners can engage with new ideas and information by connecting them to their experience with mass media, digital technology, and popular culture.

Take a look at the Media Literacy Remote Control, which offers one simple way to visualize the practice of the close analysis of text. In order to illustrate the practice of critical thinking for children and young people, I created this remote control as a metaphor to help internalize the practice of analyzing media messages in any form—books, newspapers, magazines, the Internet, video games, movies, music, and more.

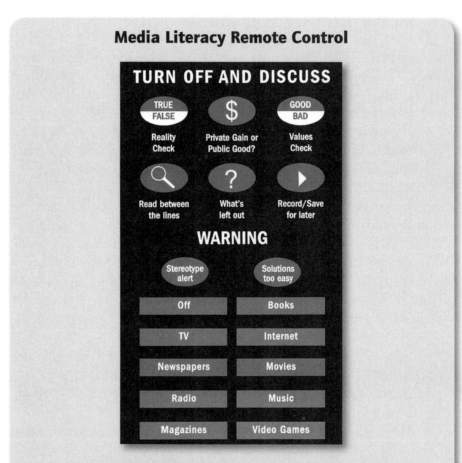

TRUE/FALSE. What's accurate and inaccurate about this message?

PRIVATE GAIN/PUBLIC GOOD. Who's making money from this message?

GOOD/BAD. How does this message relate to my values?

READ BETWEEN THE LINES. What is the implied message or subtext?

WHAT'S LEFT OUT. What information has not been included? Why?

RECORD/SAVE FOR LATER. What's valuable? What's worth remembering?

Notice two buttons on the remote control. STEREOTYPE ALERT offers a warning when people, events, or characters are presented in ways that are so typical that they seem ordinary and even banal, as when we see politicians represented in ways that make them seem phony, or blondes and athletes that are depicted as dumb. Similarly, SOLUTIONS TOO EASY warns us about oversimplifying complexity. When we read a science report, look at a dieting infomercial, listen to a radio news commentator, or check out an online political campaign message, we need to activate these critical thinking skills.

Teachers find that the remote control helps students internalize the process of asking questions and actively making interpretations. Students in one ninth-grade class in Michigan used the Media Literacy Remote Control when they were studying persuasion. As part of the unit, they analyzed a grooming product for men and a beauty product for women. The teacher used both an Old Spice commercial and a Maybelline mascara commercial to model the process of critical analysis.

The Maybelline commercial featured a bevy of beautiful young women walking smartly on a city street. There were some close-ups of their faces and reactions from observers. Catchy music and fast visual cuts made the ad compelling. At the end of the ad, a male narrator said, "Longer, thicker lashes, instantly. Maybelline." After watching the 30-second commercial, the teacher led the class in asking questions.

"What's accurate and inaccurate?" she asked.

"It says that Maybelline makes your lashes longer and thicker," said one student. "That's accurate."

"Why do you say that?" asked the teacher.

The student grinned, "I use mascara and I know that's what it does." Another chimed in somewhat deviously, "I heard mascara is made of bat poo." The class exploded in anxious laughter. Was that true? What *was* mascara made of?

The teacher assigned two students to find the answer to this question, using the computer at the back of the classroom. Within a minute or so, they determined that the bat poo story was an urban legend. Mascara is made of beeswax and other oils, they explained. "Also," one mentioned, "the Maybelline company was founded by a guy in 1913 who made mascara for his sister, Maybel."

"That's interesting! Where did that information come from?" the teacher asked. Students offered the names of the websites they had found; they had learned about source monitoring and had remembered to take note of the sources they had used. The teacher congratulated the students on their good search skills.

Together, the class looked at the ad again. "What's the implied message?" asked the teacher. "What message does this commercial state without directly saying it?"

One student raised her hand, saying, "You'll be prettier if you use this product." Another said, "You'll look more mature."

"Those are reasonable inferences," the teacher said. Then she asked, "Are there other implied messages here?"

Up went more hands. One student said, "Guys will be attracted to you if you use this product." Another pointed out, "You'll feel better about yourself if you use this product."

The teacher wrote all four ideas on the blackboard. Using pair-share, she asked students to discuss with their partner what was accurate or inaccurate about these implied messages. Within minutes, the room was buzzing. After about six minutes in active conversation with a partner, the whole class then had a robust discussion about advertising claims and their potentially positive or negative impact on the beauty ideal and self-esteem. They actively debated whether commercials are designed to make people feel inadequate in order for the company to profit. They talked about male and female gender stereotypes in advertising. When the teacher asked students to spend the last 10 minutes of class in an informal writing activity to reflect on key ideas, the room fell quiet as students began to write. Kids had a lot of ideas about grooming products, the beauty industry, advertising, and gender identity that they wanted to express. The close analysis of a familiar text served as a prewriting activity, getting them ready to develop some complex ideas in writing.

Why Critical Questions Work

It's perhaps the oldest pedagogy in existence: asking questions as a way to learn. But questioning and dialogue inevitably concern the complex relationship between teacher and student. Research shows that when teachers use questions in the classroom, they often use *closed questions*, which have only one right answer. Teachers often go fishing by asking questions that can only be answered in one way— with the right answer. Using questions to check comprehension is a common practice in the classroom, of course. But overuse of closed questions risks turning students into barking seals, performing the role of good student.

Critical questions are different because they're fundamentally interpretive—there are multiple answers possible. That's why *open-ended questions,* followed up with lots of *requests for elaboration,* are powerful. Requesting elaboration means asking, "Tell me more," "Why do you think so?" or "What's your reasoning?" to get more explicit information from students. The Common Core State Standards emphasize this process in their speaking and listening standards. Active discussion in one-on-one, small-group, and whole-class settings helps students collaborate to answer questions, build understanding, and solve problems.

Media Literacy and Inquiry Learning: Some Theory

When digital and media literacy educators began to see themselves as a learning community, it became obvious that there was a set of shared ideas that unified their interests in teaching and learning. Despite their diverse backgrounds in communication, literary theory, cultural studies, education, technology, information science, public health, and other disciplines, "continuities and correspondences began to emerge out of the most diverse practices and contexts."[3]

By 1985, media literacy educators had developed a shared theoretical framework, which helped teachers and students make sense of the field. The theory included key ideas from scholarship in literary theory, media studies, and other fields. Len Masterman pinpointed the first key idea—the concept of *constructedness.*

He noted that "the media are symbolic (or sign) systems which need to be actively read, and are not unproblematic, self-explanatory reflections of external reality. . . . The media are actively involved in processes of constructing or representing 'reality' rather than simply transmitting or reflecting it." Henry Jenkins named it the "transparency problem,"[4] and people in other fields have used still other terms for this idea. It stands first on the list of the *core concepts* of media literacy. These concepts have been articulated by a number of scholars and teachers over many years with slight differences in nuance and emphasis. My version of these concepts includes these ideas:

1. Media messages are constructed.

2. Messages are produced within economic, social, political, historical, and aesthetic contexts.

3. The process of message interpretation consists of an interaction between the reader, the text, and the culture.

4. Media use language and other symbol systems with codes and conventions associated with different genres and forms of communication.

5. Media representations play a role in people's understanding of and participation in social reality.

6. Media messages reflect and shape individual and social behavior, attitudes, and values.

In addition to exploration of these ideas, media literacy education includes a focus on pedagogy. It has deep roots in *inquiry learning.* Good learners are always learning—by asking questions, seeking out new ideas, and making connections between ideas and actions in the real world. In the inquiry approach, teachers talk to students mostly by questioning, and especially by asking *divergent questions.* These types of questions help teachers solicit a wide range of ideas, encouraging students to recognize the multiplicity of possible responses to a question. They make "I wonder . . ." statements. When students respond to questions, they do not accept short, simple answers to questions. These types of questions encourage students to interact directly with one another and avoid judging responses in order to promote risk taking and creativity in student interactions.[5]

Because most people use mass media, digital media, and popular culture as entertainment, we are used to engaging with these texts at a very superficial level. That's why the practice of close reading or close analysis can be a powerful tool to understand how media are constructed and how media texts construct reality.

Close analysis is a time-honored practice of literary analysis. The analyst or reader engages in multiple readings or viewings of the text and looks at its social and historical contexts. For some readers, it may be useful to deconstruct the text using a variety of theoretical lenses including Marxism, feminism, poststructuralism, postmodernism, psychoanalysis, and so forth. But these theoretical perspectives bring their own baggage and may not be appropriate for use with many high school students. Even for college students, students may "parrot" the teacher's pet interest in theory, instead of engaging fully in the critical analysis process.[6]

Digital and media literacy education offers concepts that work to deepen students' critical thinking and communication skills. Cary Bazalgette of the British Film Institute was the first to identify broad categories of inquiry focusing on authors, audiences, messages, language, values, and representation. These ideas are powerful working principles that apply to all textual forms—print, images, sound, and digital media—and all genres or types of expression, including user-generated content and process-based interactive media.

Five Critical Questions	
Core Concepts	*Critical Questions*
Authors and Audiences	1. Who is the author and what is the purpose?
Messages and Meanings	2. What creative techniques are used to attract and hold attention? 3. How might different people understand this message?
Representation and Reality	4. What lifestyles, values, and points of view are represented? 5. What is omitted?

Collapsed into three broad categories, critical questions address the concepts of Authors and Audiences, Messages and Meanings, and Representation and Reality. These concepts support the reading, writing, and composition process. At the end of this chapter, see the lesson plan for using critical questions to analyze any type of media text, from pages in a textbook, works of classic literature, news and current events, song lyrics, TV shows, video games, or online social interaction. But first, let's look into each of the concepts in more detail:

Authors and Audiences. When students compose, they take on the power of authorship. When they read, they stand in the position of active audience member. Many of the media texts we encounter are created by a collaborative team, working in highly capitalized industries including those in Hollywood (film), Madison Avenue (advertising), or Silicon Valley (video games and the Internet). Other times, authors are people we know, our friends and family who send us text messages, post photos on Facebook, or write e-mails. Rather than seeing authorship as only restricted to the industry of book publishing, we consider the full range of creative practices and norms used to compose messages—formally or informally, using language, images, magazines, academic writing, photography, graphic design, video game production, narrative storytelling, journalism, websites, and many other forms.

Just as authorship can be defined broadly, the concept of audiences is also broadly defined. Communication doesn't exist without an audience (a receiver, a reader, a viewer, a listener, or a user). When we read a work of classic literature, contemporary audiences make a connection across time and space with authors long dead. Audiences never know for certain about the author's intended purposes and goals; we must make *inferences* from clues provided in the text and our understanding of the historical context. Thinking about the relationship between authors and their audiences also involves consideration of ethical and social responsibilities. As a member of a particular audience, I'm aware that my attention has economic value in the marketplace and that media industries buy and sell my attention. Mass media authors sometimes make (sometimes stereotypical) assumptions about my own demographic characteristics as an older, affluent, white female, just as other authors make assumptions about what urban African American teens ages 12–17 will value.

Messages and Meanings. When students compose, they create messages; when they interpret messages, they construct meaning. The work that authors do is reflected in their choices—authors create messages through construction, carefully considering many elements in putting together a message. The work that audiences do is reflected in their interpretations—audiences create meanings. Production and reception are linked together because each is a type of creative construction process, as authors *encode* by creating messages and audiences *decode* through making interpretations and creating meanings.

Messages in every genre and form use a set of *codes and conventions* that create expectations for audiences in their process of interpreting messages. Good readers adjust their *expectations* based on the genre and form of the expression. The meaning-making process I use in reading poetry is different than the approach I use in viewing a newspaper photograph, watching a reality TV show, reading a novel, playing a video game, or listening to an audiobook. Because meaning is variable and media messages can affect our head, heart, and spirit, it's important to assess the *potential effects* of media messages as they impact individuals, groups, and society. Media messages can have variable and unexpected effects as a result of differences in meaning and interpretation. Some messages that are innocuous to some people can be destructive or hurtful to the human spirit of others.

Representation and Reality. When students compose, they depict aspects of both their life experience and their media experience. The power of communication comes from the way that messages represent reality in some way. We can judge or evaluate the quality of a message by examining how faithfully it represents some aspect of our life experience. For example, I might compare a movie that features a graduation ceremony to graduations that I have experienced as a student, a parent, and a faculty member. Even when I lack personal experience, I still evaluate the realism of a message, often by comparing one media message to another. For example, I've never been to India. But I may judge the realism of the film, *Slumdog Millionaire,* by comparing and contrasting its representation of an urban slum to articles I read in the *New York Times* about poverty in India's cities and rural areas. Because media representations stand in for my lack of direct experience, they can truly be said to "create the world." That's the major source of media's political, economic, and cultural power.

Over time, representations that become familiar through constant reuse come to feel "natural" and unmediated. But media messages are always *selective and incomplete.* That's why noticing *omissions* can help people recognize the way messages selectively represent the world, which becomes a process for recognizing how social, political, and economic power are maintained through media and communication technologies. When teachers apply these concepts in the classroom, the results can be powerful.

Grade 7 Public Speaking: What's Realistic and Unrealistic

Chet Jankowski, a middle-school teacher in North Carolina, was working on public speaking with his seventh-grade students. With 25 students, he needed to get the kids up on their feet before the class in a way that made effective use of class time. He knew that most of the anxiety and fear of public speaking was the result of not being confident about the content. When students have to make speeches about new and unfamiliar topics, they can be paralyzed with anxiety. So he created an assignment where students made short informal speeches about familiar topics and then took questions from the audience. In this assignment, students were to select a specific media message from a book, a television show, a movie, a video game, or a website that they considered realistic or unrealistic and explain their reasoning to their peers. Students had to anticipate and effectively answer listener concerns and counterarguments.

To get ready for this project, students had begun by playing some games to explore the concept of realism, picking names of TV shows out of a hat and placing them on a continuum of realistic to unrealistic, offering reasons for their answer. That lesson was described in my book, *Reading the Media: Media Literacy in High School English.*[7] Mr. Jankowski modeled an example of the assignment by giving a little speech himself, calling attention to its four-part structure and asking students to evaluate his speech using the grading rubric (discussed later). He even used one of his own favorite shows, *Star Trek.* Here's the gist of his speech:

Introduction. When I put my fingers like this (makes a hand gesture), you know what it means: Live Long and Prosper. That's what it means in Vulcan culture. They are a race of people that are depicted on *Star Trek.* It was one of my favorite shows when I was younger. In this speech, I'll explain why some aspects of *Star Trek* are realistic and other parts are unrealistic.

Description. *Star Trek* is set in the future, in the 23rd century. The TV series features the adventures of the USS *Enterprise,* a starship that explores the galaxy. By the 23rd century, humans have made alliances with people from other planets, including Vulcan. But they have made enemies with people on other planets, too. The captain is James T. Kirk and his second officer is Mr. Spock, who is half-Vulcan and half-human.

Evaluation. Because it's science fiction, there are many things about the show that people would say are unrealistic. To move from place to place, people use a transporter, which converts a person's energy into little pieces and then moves it to another location, where the energy is rematerialized. That's not a technology that exists in the real world, obviously, because it's impossible to break down energy into pieces that small and then reassemble them. But some parts of *Star Trek* do seem realistic. The characters themselves are very believable. Each one is a complicated personality. When they make decisions to help each other in a crisis, to fight with each other, or to protect each other, it seems like these feelings and situations could happen in real life, especially considering they are a group of people who work together in a very intense job.

Conclusion. Science fiction shows like *Star Trek* can seem realistic because of the personal relationships that are depicted. But lots of the actual science ideas on this show are unrealistic. But this show makes me wonder about new technologies that don't exist (but might, someday).

To prepare their own speeches, students needed to first select an appropriate media text and get approval from their teacher. Then they used class time to complete a worksheet that asked them to do the following:

- Describe the media text so that a person who is unfamiliar with it can understand it.
- Display a single PowerPoint slide with a relevant image.
- Evaluate specific realistic and unrealistic aspects of the text and offer an explanation using at least two "because" statements that include specific details.

This work served to help students plan their short speeches, which were intended to be only 1–2 minutes in length. Mr. Jankowski wanted to have time for comments and questions from listeners. Students did their speeches on all kinds of media texts, including books like *Catching Fire* by Suzanne Collins and *Jumping Off Swings* by Jo Knowles, video games like *Madden NFL 11* and *Call of Duty*; TV shows like *iCarly, The Proud Family, House,* and *Chopped*; music from artists including Lady Gaga and Justin Bieber; and movies like *Hitch, Sherlock Holmes,* and *The Pursuit of Happyness.* Because Mr. Jankowski was unfamiliar with many of the media texts students wanted to use, he learned about many new aspects of media and popular culture from his students; he also gained insight into the children from seeing the choices they made.

Each student responded to questions from listeners, who were evaluated on the quality of their questions (to discourage potential silliness and disruption). Some asked the critical questions from the Media Literacy Remote Control and others made up their own questions based on their own experience and opinions. Even the shyest student was able to demonstrate some success! Mr. Jankowski used this rubric to give students immediate feedback on their performance.

Assessing Student Oral Presentations

	Beginning	Developing	Accomplished	Exemplary
Content	Description is unclear with no evidence of reasoning	Description is clear but reasoning is hard to understand	Description is clear and reasoning is clearly presented	Description is vivid and compelling and reasoning is persuasive
Speaking	Not loud enough, uses "filler" sounds, pacing slow, relies on notes	Loud enough but some "filler" sounds and pacing problems	Loud enough, good pacing, and no reliance on notes	Loud enough, good pacing, no reliance on notes, and good vocal energy
Order	No introduction or conclusion	Introduction or conclusion but not both	Introduction, transitions, and conclusion	Attention-getting introduction, transitions. and memorable conclusion
Media	Image does not add value	Image has some value	Well-chosen image	Image is well-chosen and helps keep audience interest
Q&A	Hesitation, defensiveness	Some hesitation	Responds to questions well	Responds well and makes a connection to a key idea from the presentation

Media Literacy as the New Humanities

Teaching and learning involves genuine dialogue. Digital and media literacy education emphasizes personal agency and an awareness of the way symbols are used to construct culture. It cultivates a deep appreciation of history, economics, technology, and politics as forms of social power. That's why Ernest James Wilson, III, dean of the Annenberg School for Communication and Journalism at the University of Southern California, has called media literacy "the new humanities education."[8]

Digital and media literacy education reflect a deeply humanistic idea of education. When teachers and learners are both required to "invest something of themselves" in learning, this results in personal fulfillment and genuine receptivity to new ideas.[9] That's why we must respect students' engagement with mass media and celebrity culture. As with the humanities, digital and media literacy education helps to integrate the academic disciplines by promoting these core competencies:

Curiosity. Students engage with ideas and information to search out and find issues that matter to them. They dig in deep on things that stimulate their curiosity.

Asking Questions. Students use, find, and analyze messages to learn and identify author, audience, purpose, point of view, representation, reality, and subtext. They consider the relationship among the message's content, form, context, and culture.

Interpretation. Students consider how their understanding of a message is shaped by their own prior knowledge, attitudes, and values. They value the interpretations of others and respect the ways in which meaning is shaped through interpretation.

Synthesis. Students make connections between past and present, thinking about ideas across subject areas, and noticing patterns, parallels, consensus, and contradictions.

Expression. Students share what they learn using language, sound, images, graphics, and interactive media, appreciating the aesthetic and technical choices involved in composition. They create messages for authentic audiences to discover the power of communication as a means of social and civic action.

CHAPTER 3 LESSON PLAN

Five Critical Questions

Overview: Students work collaboratively to analyze a short media text. They discover that meaning is deepened and reshaped and new ideas are developed through curiosity, asking questions, making interpretations, attempting synthesis, and expressing ideas through dialogue.

Time: One class period

Resources Needed: A short media text in any form or genre (i.e., movie excerpt, TV commercial, magazine article or news story, print ad, website, video game, pop music, etc.), copies of the "Five Critical Questions" worksheet on page 66

Learning Outcomes:

- Appreciate the process of asking questions as a way to actively interpret a text.
- Strengthen listening and small-group discussion skills.
- Use reasoning to defend or justify an interpretation.
- Practice note taking as a way to organize and examine relationships among ideas.
- Build awareness of discussion as a form of prewriting.
- Strengthen public speaking and writing competencies.

Introduction: Preview the activity by explaining that students develop deeper meanings when analyzing any type of media message by using small-group discussion to develop and capture key ideas.

Time to Read, View, or Listen. Provide time to read, view, or listen to the text, and ask general questions such as these: "What feelings did you experience?" and "What did you like or dislike?" Encourage students to use full sentences instead of one-word answers and ask "why" questions to elicit more elaborated responses. Offer warm feedback to encourage students to contribute. Do not offer commentary or criticism of weak or poorly developed ideas.

Summarize. Pass out copies of the worksheet. Students work together to compose a summary, which should include a thesis statement and a description of key ideas. A summary should be able to stand alone as a condensed version of the original.

Repeated Reading, Viewing, or Listening. Break students into groups of two or three. Each team should tackle all five critical questions.

Small-Groups Report. Encourage groups to offer their responses to one of the five critical questions. After each group answers the question, invite other groups to add additional points or share related ideas. At this point, you should ask "why" questions to encourage students to use reasoning to explain or justify their interpretations. Through this process, the quality of ideas will deepen and students will recognize how sharing and questioning interpretations contribute to developing new ideas.

Model the Note-Taking Process. Use the board to model the note-taking process as students share their ideas and interpretations. Show students visually how ideas connect to each other.

Synthesis. Offer some reflections about your opinions regarding the most interesting ideas that develop from the analysis. Using the student comments, create a thesis statement that represents a synthesis of the best ideas that were developed in the process. Write it on the board. Explain that the process of sharing interpretations is what contributes to the development of new ideas.

Five Critical Questions

SUMMARIZE. Describe the text:

_____
_____
_____
_____

ANALYZE USING FIVE CRITICAL QUESTIONS

Who is the author and what is the purpose?

_____
_____

What techniques are used to attract and hold your attention?

_____
_____

What lifestyles, values, and points of view are represented?

_____
_____

How might different people interpret this message?

_____
_____

What is omitted?

_____
_____

A full-sized reproducible of this worksheet can be found at www.corwin.com/medialiteracy

4

The Power of Representation

What You'll Find in This Chapter:

- A high school history teacher uses critical questions to examine the representation of media images of Martin Luther King, Jr.
- When students learn how meaning and interpretation exist within specific historical and cultural contexts, they experience an increased awareness of the relationship between meaning making and various forms of social and political power.
- Language and other symbol systems represent our experience of the world, enabling us to share and learn from each other. But the representations people create are inevitably selective and incomplete.
- Visual, digital, and mass media materials now stand alongside print and literacy works as rich and complex resources that promote learning.
- Digital and media literacy education helps build alignment between learning objectives, instructional practices, and assessment.

Lesson Plan:

Exploring Point of View Through Creative Writing About History

When Linda DeCordova got an e-mail about a new curriculum resource for teaching about Martin Luther King, Jr., the timing couldn't have been more perfect. It was nearly February. Black History Month is a tradition in American education that stretches back to 1926, thanks to Dr. Carter G. Woodson. He was the historian and author (the second African American to earn a Harvard PhD) who established Negro History Week in February, to coincide with the birthdays of Abraham Lincoln and Frederick Douglass. Mrs. DeCordova clicked on the link, reviewed the curriculum materials, and decided to try them out with her students since she had to cover the civil rights movement eventually that term.

Like many history teachers, Mrs. DeCordova was known for her intense love of her subject and her substantial emphasis on content. As she explains, there's simply so much knowledge that's needed to understand our past that she has to lecture. In order to make history more accessible to her high school students, she used film and video resources frequently in her classes. She had used videos about the civil rights movement that she had obtained from United Streaming and found samples of local TV news programs, in her home state of Virginia, about the coverage of the civil rights movement during the 1950s and 1960s. In the early 1990s she had used films like *Mississippi Burning,* a film loosely based on the FBI investigation into the real-life murders of three civil rights workers in the U.S. state of Mississippi in 1964. But over the years, she had noticed that the film seemed to be less effective with her students, who seemed almost bored by it. Perhaps students took their cues from her, as she was also a little tired of showing it year after year.

These new curriculum materials she reviewed, created by Project Look Sharp at Ithaca College, seemed easy enough to implement with just a little previewing. There was plenty of room for her to add her own knowledge of the civil rights movement, too. This curriculum was certainly not intimidating—not like some other history curriculum materials developed by university faculty who perhaps weren't so familiar with the nature of the average American 15-year-old.

The curriculum, titled *Media Constructions of Martin Luther King, Jr.* (available at www.ithaca.edu/looksharp), did more than offer historical information and resources for teaching about King's contribution to the civil rights movement in the United States. It also aimed to teach students to analyze *how* the portrayal of Dr. King has been constructed differently through various media forms, depending upon who was doing the constructing, for what purpose, for what audience, and with what bias. Lessons and activities emphasized the skills of critical reading of images, including comic book covers, billboards, newspaper articles, speeches, logos and buttons, book covers, magazine articles, documentary and fictional films about the time period, and music videos about civil rights. The first set of lessons Mrs. DeCordova used involved students responding to a series of historical and contemporary images using critical questions.

Analysis in Action: Using Critical Questions

Authors and Audiences

- Who produced this document, and for what purpose?
- When was this produced, and what was its historical context?
- Who is the target audience?

Messages and Meanings

- What are the messages communicated?
- What techniques are used to attract and hold attention?
- How might different people interpret this message differently?
- Who might benefit from (and who might be harmed by) this message?

Representation and Reality

- What information or perspective is left out of this message?
- Is this an accurate and credible representation?
- How does this reflect the perspective or bias of its creator?

One at a time, Mrs. DeCordova presented her students with images of the covers of four *Time* magazine covers from 1957, 1964, 1965, and 2006 (shown in Figure 4.1), all featuring images of Martin Luther King. She asked these open-ended questions, encouraging students to use clues in the images and their background knowledge of the time period to support their ideas.

"What messages are communicated by these images?" asked Mrs. DeCordova.

One student explained, "He's all alone in these covers, and he looks troubled. See that long shadow behind him in the cover from 1964? And the image from 1965 is a little weird. Is it making fun of him?"

"I wonder if this is a caricature," responded Mrs. DeCordova, writing the word on the board. "A caricature is a picture that emphasizes certain features of a person, to make them look funny."

Heads nodded. Students could see that perhaps the 1965 *Time* magazine image was a caricature. But then William, a student who

Figure 4.1   Media Constructions of
Martin Luther King, Jr.

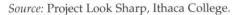

Source: Project Look Sharp, Ithaca College.

rarely spoke in class, raised his hand. "See this question, 'What techniques are used to attract your attention?' The style of drawing looks like a sketch done of someone who's moving around. The artist makes King look like he's in the middle of a speech, or a march or something."

Students turned to look at William. More heads nodded. "Good point," one kid said, acknowledging William.

Another girl echoed the idea, "Yeah, it looks like he's not just sitting around—he's in the middle of a march or something." But then she added, "Didn't he march on Washington in 1965?" This student was attempting to connect the representation to reality, Mrs. DeCordova thought to herself. It's the first time she's spoken in class all week—and she's on task!

The teacher offered a small correction—King delivered his "I Have a Dream" speech in 1963 in front of 300,000 people gathered at the National Mall in Washington, DC. During this time, King was helping to organize voter registration programs throughout the South, and nonviolent protesters continued to meet violent resistance from police. Then, in March 1965, in the town of Selma, Alabama, state troopers and local police attacked peaceful demonstrators with billy clubs, tear gas, rubber tubes wrapped in barbed wire, and bull whips. The national broadcast of peaceful marchers seeking the right to vote and being attacked by police horrified the nation.

Instead of continuing to lecture, Mrs. DeCordova repeated the open-ended prompt question: "In this image, what techniques are used to attract and hold your attention?" She paused. Just as she was about to move on, another voice piped up from the back of the room. "Doesn't his skin look darker in the 1965 image, as compared to earlier images?" said Janine. Janine was African American. Then another student asked, "Were white people beginning to be more afraid of Dr. King's efforts to give black people equal rights?" Then there erupted a little hubbub of conversation, as several students turned to each other to comment on these new observations and questions.

The teacher regained control of the class and complimented students on these points: "We could look at the news media of the time period to understand the question about white people's increased fear during the 1960s." After the Civil Rights Act was passed in 1964, people recognized the need to address the problem of inequity in education. But when busing was used to achieve racial equality, many white people were opposed to the plan. Racism takes many forms, of course, and people may be overtly racist or have biases that they are unaware of, she explained.

Mrs. DeCordova then used her whiteboard to take students to Project Implicit (www.projectimplicit.com), a web research site that demonstrates the difference between people's conscious and unconscious bias by measuring their reaction times while categorizing different images. She encouraged students to explore the site at home to discover more about their conscious and unconscious biases.

Even today, she told students, the lightness or darkness of skin tone may unconsciously shape and reflect people's opinions about a political figure. She recalled a *Newsweek* article she had read about an experiment from researchers at the University of Chicago that showed that political partisanship affects perception. Researchers took three images of President Obama in different settings and created a lightened and darkened version of each so they had a total of nine images. In the study, a large group of people were asked about their political attitudes and then randomly exposed to three of the nine images and asked to rate the appeal of the images. Regardless of the pose or setting of the image, liberals preferred the lightened image and conservatives preferred the darker image.[1] People of all races can be affected by this.

So, Mrs. DeCordova concluded, it's important to be aware of your own interpretations and to make every effort to heighten your consciousness about how you are seeing things. As she looked out at the attentive faces in front of her, she realized that connecting the historical lesson on Martin Luther King, Jr., to present-day issues of unconscious bias had increased students' engagement in the learning process.

Teaching Representation

Everything that we know comes from one of two sources: direct, real-world experience or mediated experience. By this I mean *symbol systems* of one kind or other. It's why people can become fascinated with language, media, and technology in all its many forms.

Since the world as I experience it each day is pretty limited, I depend upon messages created by others for much of my understanding of the world.

Through language, for example, I get access to other people's direct, real-world experience. When a friend tells me stories about her trip to Las Vegas or Miami, I can share in some part of what it was like for her. But no matter how many rich details she offers about her experience, listening to the story is not the same as having the direct experience myself. But still, I learn a lot from listening to her travel adventures. An author's choices shape and frame a learning experience in amazing ways. A good storyteller can make experience come alive in my mind, but a poor storyteller will simply bore me.

Language is the most fundamental symbol system of humanity and every student needs to appreciate how powerful it is in shaping our understanding of ourselves and the world around us.

We Learn From Experience

Direct, Real-World Experience	Mediated Experience
Cooking	Reading
Walking Around the Neighborhood	Viewing Pictures and Moving Images
Making Music	Listening to Music
Learning to Drive	Playing Games and Using Interactive Media

It's worth reflecting on just how deep and profound our dependence on others really is. There are many things that I claim to "know" that I know *only* from mediated experience. In fact, most of what I know about the world comes from media sources—from stories people have told me or from reading and viewing. For example, I've never been arrested or in prison. Yet I have some clear and vivid understanding of what that might be like. When I ask my students about what it's like to be arrested, they can tell me about the whole process: from the arrest to the ride in the police car to the plea bargain. I can mentally visualize what the lockup experience might be like, and I have expectations about how I might react physically and mentally. Entertaining books, movies, and TV shows have been a powerful source of information for me about the world of crime and law enforcement.

This is part of the reason why so many people love video games. Many video games offer users a set of choices that closely model the many choices we face in direct, real-world experience. The *immersion* we experience when "it feels so real" is captivating and pleasurable because it closely approximates lived experience.

We make choices every moment of the day. But it's important to recognize how choice is structured, both in real life and in video games. No one is ever completely free to make choices. Just as our social roles and the social institutions around us structure the choices we can make in the real world, we must consider *how choices are structured* by the storyteller and the game-design team when we play video games.

When humans started writing down their stories about 5,000 years ago, we extended our power to share experience across time and space. This rapidly increased our ability to learn from each other. But just as my own direct, real-world experience of the world is selective and incomplete because of my perception and interpretation processes, media representations are also inevitably selective and incomplete. Authors make choices when representing their experience and imagination using symbols. Many of the stories of the historical past represent the point of view of the winners—those who were at the top of the social, political, and cultural hierarchy.

I hope it's clear that the topic of representation-reality isn't just relevant to history teachers, who have a deep stake in understanding the complexity and nuances of the historical past. The representation-reality issue is vital for the fields of literature, science, health, and math, too. For example, William Faulkner offered us a representation of family life in his novel, *As I Lay Dying.* He captures something complicated, awful, and profound about the ways our feelings about our family members and relatives shape the choices we make throughout the life span. In the book, *On the Origin of Species,* Charles Darwin offered us a representation of biological life that provides a powerful explanation for the diversity of species over time. Mathematics is the best example of a powerful representational system—perhaps the most abstract of all—that people use to understand some aspects of reality. Through statistics, linear modeling, and other mathematical techniques, we can "see" the underlying organizational principles that explain many aspects of the physical and cultural world.

> ### How Representations Shape
> ### Our Understanding of the World
>
> **Step 1.** Authors experience the world.
>
> **Step 2.** Authors construct messages using symbol systems to represent their ideas, thoughts, and feelings. Messages are representations of authors' experience of the world.
>
> **Step 3.** Audiences interpret meaning from messages they encounter. Meanings are audiences' interpretations of the messages authors create.
>
> **Step 4.** Audiences rely on representations to make judgments and inferences about social reality.

Using Media Texts as Objects of Study

In recent years, social studies educators have placed an increasing emphasis on developing teaching strategies to help students learn to think like historians. This means less focus on "covering" material through lecturing and more focus on "uncovering" the process of critically analyzing, comparing, and synthesizing texts to form meaningful interpretations of the historical past.[2] Mrs. DeCordova was really working to develop this approach. Still, she did often use lecture/dictation, where students listened and took notes, as part of her teaching. She considered her U.S. history course as a way for her students to develop functional civic knowledge about the American political, economic, and social systems. She had experimented with the use of primary source documents and had tried to include more writing in addition to multiple-choice tests and quizzes. But those practices were often labor-intensive and sometimes exhausting as she taught over 110 students per semester.

Like many teachers, Mrs. DeCordova was well aware of how much of her students' knowledge about history was shaped by mass media and popular culture, as well as family and peers. In her world history course last year, she spent some time exploring the accuracies and inaccuracies in the film *300* about the Battle of Thermopylae. Students gained a lot of information about the Spartan culture and values from watching that film.

But as a result of this experience with the Project Look Sharp curriculum, Mrs. DeCordova began to realize something about herself: She had generally tended to view film and video resources as a means to enhance students' knowledge, not to promote critical analysis skills. In the lesson she had just taught, the images of Martin Luther King, Jr., were used as objects of study, not just as illustrations or pretty pictures associated with the historical content.

The critical questions used in this activity were fundamentally different from the questions she usually asked, which Mrs. DeCordova saw as recall questions and critics would call "guess-what-I'm thinking" questions.[3] In general, after viewing images, video, and film clips about U.S. history, Mrs. DeCordova's approach involved asking students questions where they had to describe or summarize the material. With this approach, there really was only one right answer to each question, and so most of her students just waited patiently for one of a small handful of kids to answer it. Only rarely were there differences in students' interpretation of the kind that the teacher was observing when she used the Project Look Sharp curriculum.

As British media literacy scholar Len Masterman has pointed out, the attitude that media and technology are simply an aid to learning or tools for disseminating knowledge and experience is the biggest challenge in using media and technology in education. This approach conceptualizes media and technology as either neutral transmitters of ideas and information, as good educational source materials suitable for classroom learning, or as noneducational escapism or low-quality trash that need not be taken seriously at all. These perspectives on the use of media and technology in education are the very antithesis of digital and media literacy education.[4]

In the following days, they finished the lesson by comparing and contrasting three short film clips featuring Dr. Martin Luther King, Jr., and Malcolm X, from the documentary film, *Eyes on the Prize,* the feature film, *Malcolm X,* featuring Denzel Washington, and *King,* a TV miniseries, all provided in the Project Look Sharp curriculum. Here the conversation delved into the concept of nonviolent resistance and how it has been portrayed in the media. Students were genuinely torn about the pros and cons of nonviolent resistance—some students considered it to be a noble and inspirational effort while others, echoing the arguments of Malcolm X, found it a little cowardly and self-defeating. Now attentive to the constructed nature of media representations, they understood how the characteristics of a professional actor, like Denzel Washington, might be able to make the statements of Malcolm X seem more appealing because of the quality of his acting performance.

Students responded well to open-ended questions where there was no right or wrong answers and where differences in student interpretation sometimes created surprising new insights. Over the next few days, the teacher used other lesson plans from the curriculum, including an activity where students compare and contrast three Martin Luther King, Jr., speeches, including three famous speeches from 1963, 1967, and 1968. When she handed out a short reading with comprehension questions for homework, there was none of the usual grumbling. They *wanted* to learn more about Martin Luther King, Malcolm X, and the civil rights movement. Why? More knowledge would help them develop and share more sophisticated interpretations.

Connecting Learning Across the Disciplines

In the lunchroom, Mrs. DeCordova had heard the English department chairman talking about the efforts at the Virginia Department of Education to include media literacy into the state's English curriculum. The big change, it seemed, involved including visual, digital, and mass media materials alongside the printed work, using the more general word "text" instead of the terms "literary works" or "print." In January 2010, the Virginia Board of Education revised the English Language Arts curriculum to include the following standards for students in Grade 10 English:

The student will read and analyze texts of different cultures and eras.

- Explain the influence of historical context on the form, style, and point of view of a literary text.
- Evaluate how an author's choices shape the intended meaning of a text.
- Compare and contrast how rhyme, rhythm, sound, imagery, style, form, and other literacy devices convey a message and elicit a reader's emotions.

The student will analyze, produce, and examine similarities and differences between visual and verbal messages.

- Use media, visual literacy, and technology skills to create products.
- Evaluate sources including advertisements, editorials, blogs, Web sites, and other media for relationships between intent, factual content, and opinion.
- Determine the author's purpose and intended effect on the audience for media messages.
- Identify the tools and techniques used to achieve the intended focus.[5]

These standards are at the heart of digital and media literacy education. But in considering how to assess student learning, Mrs. DeCordova knew that multiple-choice exams, identification items, or straight essay exams all simply reward students for memorization and encourage them to copy or imitate information provided by the teacher. Those were not the competencies for democratic citizenship that she was aiming to develop.

She wanted assessment that would demonstrate her students' ability to identify, analyze, and interpret primary and secondary source materials; evaluate the authenticity, authority, and credibility of sources; communicate findings orally and in analytical essays and/or comprehensive papers; develop skills in discussion, debate, and persuasive writing with respect to enduring issues and determine how divergent viewpoints have been addressed and reconciled; and interpret the significance of excerpts from famous speeches and other documents.[6]

Here was an alignment opportunity, a way to make her learning outcomes line up with her assessment strategies. Working with the English department chairman to create the assignment, she decided to end the unit on the civil rights movement with a writing activity, something that she rarely had time to do with her five classes. In collaboration with her colleague in the English department, she asked students to compose a historical dialogue that included two people's different points of view about Martin Luther King, Jr., and the civil rights movement. See the assignment, which can be found at the end of this chapter.

To explore how point of view shapes the constructions of history, professor David Voelker uses a "For and Against" activity with students in his introductory college history classes, asking students to respond critically to a set of historical claims, such as "The U.S. Constitution created a democratic government" or "The antebellum Republican Party posed a serious threat to the institution of slavery." Students write two brief paragraphs that provide the best evidence for the statement and the best evidence against the statement, with three or four pieces of evidence for each side. Voelker explains as follows:

They have to show not only that they have information to bring to bear on the statement but also that they can evaluate the statement as a historian by judging historical significance, recognizing complexity and contingency, and drawing on context and chronology to frame their explanations. Each time they respond to a statement, students fashion rudimentary historical arguments by transforming inert facts into applied evidence.[7]

By applying media literacy pedagogy to social studies, Mrs. DeCordova discovered that this approach fits naturally within the state's curriculum framework for teaching U.S. history because of its emphasis on critical analysis, which demands authentic thinking by requiring students to carry out the kind of task—evaluating claims and using evidence—that they will regularly encounter in life outside of the classroom.

CHAPTER 4 LESSON PLAN

Exploring Point of View
Through Creative Writing About History

Overview: After comparing and contrasting excerpts of Dr. Martin Luther King's speeches—"I Have a Dream" (1963), "Beyond Vietnam" (1967), or the "Mountaintop" speech (1968)—write a short script set in 1968, featuring two people who listened to all three speeches but have different opinions about Martin Luther King. Before writing, gather information about the time period in order to make the dialogue more believable and authentic.

Step 1: Watch and Listen. Review the three excerpts of the Martin Luther King speeches that we viewed and discussed in class, which are available here: http://www.ithaca.edu/looksharp/?action=mlk

Pay attention to the rhyme, rhythm, metaphors, and emotional tone used in each excerpt and take notes that capture the most important passages.

Step 2: Create Characters. Develop plausible characters in a specific situation from any time period between 1968 and 1972. Your script *must* include at least one of the following characters:

- A news reporter
- A supporter of civil rights
- Someone who opposed civil rights
- A police officer who was assigned to crowd control during the 1964 riots
- A soldier in Vietnam
- A striking Memphis sanitation worker
- A political leader
- A member of the clergy

Step 3: Create a Plausible Time and Place. Use your imagination and your historical reasoning to come up with a plausible context and situation for your characters to be together. Visualize a specific place where a meaningful dialogue about Martin Luther King could take place.

Step 4: Gather Information. Gather research from a variety of sources (minimum of three). Ask your family members about their memories of 1968–1972. Check out some books about life in America during the 1960s and 1970s. Learn more about how newspapers covered the civil rights movement in your community. Take a look at some historical magazines from this period. Listen to some popular music or watch some movies from this time period that have different points of view about civil rights.

Step 5: Compose. Write a dialogue between two characters, reviewing the criteria for evaluation as you edit and revise your work before the due date.

Criteria for Evaluation

1. Your script has interesting characters and a believable setting and situation. Your characters have distinctly different points of view about Martin Luther King's role in the civil rights movement.

2. You use at least three specific passages from Martin Luther King speeches in your script.

3. Your writing shows evidence that you have considered information from class readings, viewing, and discussion.

4. Your writing shows evidence that you have gathered new information from your own independent research. List the resources you used in a reference list at the end of your dialogue.

5. You use the conventions of a script, including the following:
   - A description of setting and context at the top in *italics*
   - Character names in **bold,** followed by spoken dialogue
   - Stage directions for actors' movement and emotional expression [in brackets or *italics*]

Source: Adapted from Media Construction of Martin Luther King, Jr., Project Look Sharp (www.ithaca.edu/looksharp).

CREATE

Chapter 5. Composing With Media Across the Curriculum

5

Composing With Media Across the Curriculum

What You'll Find in This Chapter:

- A chemistry teacher helps students gain familiarity with the periodic table by having them develop an ad campaign for an element on the periodic table. When students make short films to document a lab experiment, they demonstrate an understanding of the scientific process and gain awareness of the constructed nature of visual media.
- Creative multimedia composition assignments, like the "Why?" video project, include a mix of structure and freedom to provide optimal support for creativity, self-expression, and success.
- Educators need to be attentive to how the phases of romance, precision, and generalization help support the development of students' intellectual curiosity.
- Creating a documentary offers unexpected teachable moments that enable the exploration of ethical issues and social responsibility.
- There are six different challenges in designing and implementing student projects that must be addressed in order to support the authentic development of student voice.

Lesson Plan:

Periodic Propaganda: A Multimedia Chemistry Project

As a teacher in an urban public school, Paul Wagenhoffer was concerned about the lack of public knowledge about science. Paul was aware that many of his students would not develop a deep appreciation for scientific ways of thinking just by focusing on the textbook and the lab experiments. He had read studies that showed that few American adults can accurately define the term "molecule."

It's no surprise that many of Mr. Wagenhoffer's students, even at age 15, had already foreclosed on science as a possible career, deciding that a job in science was not for them, in part because of influences of family and community and in part because of the negative stereotypes about scientists that are common in popular culture. Researchers have shown that children form negative images of scientists quite early on, usually by the time they reach the second grade.[1] For many of his students, chemistry was simply a required course, another hoop to jump through en route to high school graduation.

Mr. Wagenhoffer wanted to share his passion about chemistry with his students. Why? He knew that students would be using and applying chemical concepts all throughout their lives in ordinary activities like cooking and using medicines. Throughout their lifetimes, they would be benefitting from scientific innovation in chemistry, medicine, and engineering. He wanted students to be able to grow into the kinds of adults who participate in public discourse about science and technology. That means he wanted his students to have a deep understanding of how scientists conceptualize and solve problems. He knew that "without a grasp of scientific ways of thinking, the average person cannot tell the difference between science based on real data and something that resembles science—at least in their eyes—but is based on uncontrolled experiments, anecdotal evidence, and passionate assertions."[2] How could hands-on work with digital media and technology support students' appreciation of chemistry?

Periodic Propaganda: Media Production in Chemistry Class

As part of a larger plan to connect disciplines of chemistry, media arts, and graphic arts, Mr. Wagenhoffer developed a creative media production project for the first quarter of his chemistry class. Called "Periodic Propaganda," students gained familiarity with the chemical elements and deepened their understanding of the uses of the elements in daily life. Over the course of two weeks, students learned about the structure of the periodic table of elements. Each student selected an element (carbon, radium, copper, etc.) and worked independently to learn about its physical properties, its history, and its uses. Students used a worksheet to capture essential information and to document their research process by learning to cite sources.

Using creativity and imagination, as if working for an advertising agency, each student developed a way to "sell" the element by using image composition tools to create a *propaganda poster*. Then students developed a one-minute oral *persuasive pitch* to explain to listeners why their element is the best. Students also composed a two-page written report on their element, based on the independent research they conducted using library and online sources.

A sample of student-created propaganda posters for the elements plutonium, copper, xenon, and gold is shown in Figure 5.1. The student production plan is shown at the end of this chapter. The periodic table of elements is presented in an ordered and structured way that includes the atomic number, atomic mass, and element name and symbol. In this assignment, students were asked to reproduce that information, but to include a persuasive slogan and use visuals to demonstrate the element and its uses. They were asked to create a slogan or catch phrase that would catch a viewer's attention and draw it to the piece; students could be serious or humorous, but the slogan needed to make a connection to the element. The evaluation rubric for the poster included four criteria: creativity, content, following directions, and using technology well.

According to Mr. Wagenhoffer, students really enjoyed this activity. "We're a school that values integrating the arts across the curriculum,

Figure 5.1   Periodic Propaganda

and for many students, this intensified their curiosity about the periodic table." The lesson introduced them to the many fascinating dimensions of the elements, helped students gain a sense of expertise about one element, and gave them a feeling of confidence that they could explore a new topic. Intensifying curiosity is an important part of our job as educators.

Today, every teacher needs to be a media composition teacher. That's because the power of authorship offers students of all ages a transformative learning practice. When students create messages, they gain new knowledge while strengthening communication and problem-solving skills. They put knowledge into practice. When students are authors, they have authority: the Latin root shows us the connection between these two concepts. Online media composition tools, available at students' fingertips, make it easier than ever for learners to experience the power of authorship.

Visualizing the Scientific Process

Science teachers may encourage students to make short films documenting a lab experiment or any aspect of science. This learning experience can yield rich insights for students and strengthen both the understanding of the scientific process and the constructed nature of visual media. Developing and editing scientific digital videos is fun for students and it allows them to share scientific understandings and explanations.[3] It requires careful attention to planning, using multiple symbol systems including language, drawings, still and moving images—and even special effects.

British teachers Andrew Burn and James Durran describe the work of middle-school science students. Children were required to film a simple experiment from several different angles, then edit the sequence and add narration. At the beginning of the project, the teacher and students take a look at how science is represented on television and film—both in educational programs and in entertainment media. They learn that an experiment depicted on the screen is, in fact, constructed by editing together sequences from several different experiments.

The teacher presents the students with a poor-quality example of a filmed experiment, in which the camera is simply pointed at the bench while the experiment is being conducted. When students observe that the film is hard to understand, they work with a partner to plan their own strategies for making a better film.

A clearly stated purpose, a description of the materials and processes, careful observation, and clearly stated conclusions are all necessary for a film about science to accomplish its goals. Students discover that it matters where you place the camera, what materials are in the background, what words are used to describe the image, and how the sequence is edited together. Audiences may remember ideas better if powerful metaphors or humor is used strategically. As Burn and Durran put it, "Learning about science and learning about the medium [of film] have converged," since students discover that the effectiveness of their choices in filming, editing, and narration "inevitably returns to the issue of how well the scientific process is being communicated."[4]

Creativity Under Constraints

Some of the best project-based learning assignments using media and technology give students a combination of structure and freedom, where they can develop communication skills and exercise their creativity but have some constraints that limit and shape their work. At Ladue Horton Watkins High School in Saint Louis, Missouri, students may enroll in a video production course. Teams of students create short videos in their community, learning interviewing skills and designing messages for entertainment and informational purposes. Don Goble's students also produce *Ladue View*, a 40-minute television news magazine show. Students write, direct, film, edit, and produce news features, entertainment stories, sports highlights, promotional advertisements, public service announcements, and community projects on a monthly basis.

In reflecting on herself as a learner, one Ladue student explained as follows: "Though I didn't really have a choice about asking strangers their thoughts and opinions, it became somewhat natural after hours and hours of doing it. Breaking out of my comfort zone was surprisingly fun! I had a great time getting to know my classmates better and developing my skills of being on a production team."[5] Here students develop technology skills in relation to the larger focus on the development of communication competencies.

In the spring of 2010, Mr. Goble designed an assignment that invited students to create a 90-second video answering the question, "Why?" This assignment provided a good mix of creativity and constraint: There were no guidelines for content, but the production had to address the theme of "why," be exactly 90 seconds in length, and be completed by a strictly enforced deadline.

One student, determined to make a humorous point that every question can be answered, picked a random name out of the school directory, tracked down that kid, and asked him for a question to answer. The student asked the question, "Why does everyone hate Justin Bieber?" Then he edited together a playful montage of student responses ranging from "He's got a high voice," "He's really childish and annoying," to references to "his flippy hair." As a message clearly intending to entertain, the video concludes with a shot of milk cartons featuring a Justin Bieber promotion from Disney and some teen boys flipping their hair. Assignments like this that include a mix of structure and freedom provide optimal support for students' creativity and confidence as authors.

A Process for Producing the "Why?" Video

Assignment: In exactly 90 seconds, create an informative, entertaining, or persuasive video for your peers by asking a "why" question and answering it in a way that demonstrates creativity and imagination.

Preproduction

- Spend plenty of time brainstorming various "why" questions that you might explore before you settle on a specific idea.
- As you consider your target audience, make some decisions about your purpose: Will you inform, entertain, or persuade?
- Think carefully about how you might visualize both your "why" question and the process of answering it.
- Consider the constraints of your deadline and the resources you will need as you plan your project.
- Create a script that maps out what the viewer will see and hear.
- Make a production plan that lists what you'll need to do to film your project.

Production

- Gather the people and the materials you need for the production.
- Help people understand their roles and responsibilities as part of the production team.
- Rehearse and practice with your team.
- Film the shots you need, paying special attention to the sound and image quality.

(Continued)

(Continued)

Postproduction

- Review your footage carefully and make decisions about which shots to use.
- Use video editing software to assemble images and sound in sequence.
- As part of your revision process, get feedback from people who are unfamiliar with the project to see if they understand your message.
- Add transitions, titles, music, sound, or special effects if needed.
- Save a copy of your production in a file format that can be shared with others.

The term *media composition* carries a distinctly different tone and sensibility as compared with the terms *technology integration* or *digital learning* or *media production*. I've never been satisfied with those who simply use technology for technology's sake. In my view, the process of media composition has many conceptual parallels with the classic practices developed by writing teachers. According to Peter Smagorinsky, these include the following:

1. The use of an appropriate tool or set of tools

2. An understanding of the conventions and genres within which one is working and an understanding of the effects of breaking these conventions

3. An extended process that usually includes planning, drafting, feedback, reflection, and revising

4. Building on prior knowledge and understanding as a basis for the construction of new ideas and a new text

5. New learning that takes place through the process of composing

6. Rewarding both the process of composing and the ultimate texts as sources of meaning[6]

Romance, Precision, Generalization

Media composition practices promote intellectual curiosity. As a learner myself, I was lucky enough to fall in love with learning. It's been the love of my life. It was a process that I came to understand as having three phases: romance, precision, and generalization. Alfred North Whitehead, a major figure in mathematical logic, first conceptualized education in this way. Whitehead taught at Harvard University in the philosophy department for many years, writing a book called the *Aims of Education,* written in 1929. Deeply influenced by John Dewey, Whitehead was interested in the synthesis between knowledge and application in both the humanities and the sciences.

Knowledge cannot be considered separate from the context in which it is used, he argued. And teachers must be sensitive to the cycle of engagement in which learning develops.

Romance comes first. Emotional involvement with the subject matter compels our interest. Then we develop a need for *precision,* where we acquire a shared vocabulary, systematic knowledge, and an understanding of how new ideas are created within the discipline. This helps us go deeper into the learning process. Finally, *generalization* happens when we connect our romantic involvement with ideas with the precision of deeper exploration to formulate new knowledge ourselves or apply ideas in ways that are serviceable in a particular context or setting.

The cycle of romance, precision, and generalization is at the heart of the creative process in science. When chemistry professor John Berry was a fourth grader, he remembers an activity where students were asked to answer the question, "What will you be doing 20 years from now?" At age 9, he said he would be an artist, and indeed, he is—as both a chemist and a musician. In 2007, he offered a talk to Wisconsin teachers about the topic of antilogous harmony (harmony between two dissimilar things), something he describes as the chocolate-and-peanut-butter effect. He explained that creative combination drives the science of making new compounds in chemistry— and it also drives the creation of new harmonies in music. "As an inorganic chemist, I am an artist who works with the periodic table of elements," he explained.[7]

When the romance bond is strong and students are fully engaged in a topic, they are eager to delve into the precision stage of the process. But without romance, the work involved to dig into a subject can make study seem lifeless and dull. Whitehead warned educators about the danger of *inert ideas,* ideas that are merely received into the mind without being utilized, or tested, or thrown into fresh combinations. He noticed that when romance has been fully activated, ideas come alive for the learner because they are relevant and because the learner can engage with them.

Disconnected ideas, not "illuminated with any spark of vitality," promote passive reception on the part of the student. To promote the joy of discovery, Whitehead advocates what later education reform scholars like Ted Sizer and others have emphasized. Follow two educational commandments: "Do not teach too many subjects," and again, "What you teach, teach thoroughly."[8]

Whitehead spoke powerfully about the need for education to be relevant, explaining, "The only use of a knowledge of the past is to equip us for the present." He explained that the value of teaching quadratic equations, for example, is not in "sharpening the mind" for future work, as if the mind were a dead instrument. The metaphor of learning as training mental capacity is "one of the most fatal, erroneous, and dangerous conceptions ever introduced into the theory of education."[9]

Learning about life, in all its manifestations, is the only necessary subject matter for education, said Whitehead. His conceptualization of project-based learning was intuitive, simple, and richly engaging: In a math class, students can survey a field or other outdoor location, draw a plan of it to scale, and find the area. In this context, the geometrical propositions and proofs can be learned—and remembered—because the ideas were situated in the context of practical activity. Media composition projects offer this same type of practical real-world activity that promotes and sustains intellectual curiosity, collaboration, and social responsibility.

Documentary Ethics in the Classroom

It was the perfect culminating activity, thought Jay Peterson, a science teacher at Nauset High School on Cape Cod, Massachusetts. He had decided that his ninth-grade students would compose short video documentaries about the local ecosystem behind the high school, which included a wooded area and some wetlands, as part of their environmental science class. Students were encouraged to identify an environmental issue in or around the school with cultural significance. They needed to find print media sources and capture video to visualize the issue for a broad general audience. Students had a timetable for completing these projects that included a mix of in-classroom work and homework, with time for brainstorming their media productions, developing a main idea, scripting, taping, and editing. Since they only had access to one video camera, small teams of 4–5 students were assigned a particular day for shooting video. Students worked on a wide range of topics, including recycling, carbon footprints, water drainage, and so forth.

One day, a group of students came into class with a problem they wanted to discuss with Mr. Peterson. Their video was about wetlands pollution created by garbage blown from containers in the kettle pond behind their school. "There's always a mess of plastic bottles and grocery store bags and candy wrappers and stuff there," said one student. "But when we went to shoot our video yesterday, for some reason, there wasn't any garbage." Perhaps the wind had blown it to another location. "Could we fake the shot?" one kid asked. "We could put some garbage in the pond, take the video shots we need, and then clean it up."

Mr. Peterson remembers being flummoxed by the question. He was a science teacher, not a documentary filmmaker. He wasn't sure how to respond. The documentary genre has long enjoyed a privileged position because of its claim to be able to accurately capture and represent reality. But he also knew that these students grew up watching all manner of fake documentaries, including *Borat*, featuring a boorish Kazakhstani TV personality who is dispatched to the United States, and *The Blair Witch Project*, a horror film that purports to depict the experience of three student filmmakers set out into the forest to film a documentary on a legendary ghost. Mock-documentary movies demonstrate how easily and successfully documentary forms can be faked. This can subvert the special status of documentaries as a truthful genre. After all, even mainstream documentary filmmakers manipulate many aspects of reality (through editing, for example) to suit the needs of their main idea or central argument.[10]

Should student filmmakers fake the garbage shot? Mr. Peterson decided to make this ethical question a subject for classroom discussion. He asked small groups of students to develop a *pro–con* list. On the board, he wrote the words "advantages" and "disadvantages." But then Mr. Peterson asked students to adopt the point of view of one of three stakeholders who might have distinct opinions when responding to this question: scientists, filmmakers, and the audience.

When student teams shared their lists, it generated a good discussion. Mr. Peterson documented the best ideas on the blackboard, creating an informal 3×2 chart to organize the ideas, as shown in Figure 5.2. Some students viewed a fake garbage shot as doing a disservice to the audience, who were right to have a reasonable expectation

Figure 5.2   A Discussion: Should Filmmakers Fake the Garbage Shot?

Point of View	Yes	No
Scientists	It would make the film more informative.	It goes against the core values of science. Documenting what really happens is the essence of the scientific method.
Filmmakers	We have only one day to film the project. Sometimes to tell the truth you have to fake stuff.	We may be able to find other creative ways to depict the pollution.
Audience	We understand that not all images are literally true. Images are just symbols.	We expect documentaries to be truthful and to show what really exists.

that the images were accurate. Some students were sympathetic to the needs of filmmakers to want to fake the shot, persuaded by their need to complete their film under time constraints and create a compelling visual narrative. Other students were sympathetic to the perspective of scientists, who depend on shared social norms of truth-telling and accuracy as essential components of the scientific process. At the end of the period, Mr. Peterson asked students to think about which of the many ideas were most compelling and important to them personally.

In class the next day, students had plenty of interest in continuing the dialogue. A couple of kids had spontaneously investigated this topic at home, typing the words "fake shot" and "documentary" into Google to see what they could find. They found out that almost all nature documentaries use creative editing and artifice to make the show more interesting and informative. Many documentaries use techniques like *reenactment* and *spoken testimony* to visually represent scenes that are not possible to film. But such practices may stretch the link between the representation and the reality in ways that mislead and misinform viewers.

The use of computer-generated imagery (CGI) in documentaries is a case in point. There's a whole spate of documentary programs about aliens, extraterrestrials, and dragons. These subjunctive documentaries represent not actuality, but instead depict "that which could be or might have been." Shows like *Walking With Dinosaurs* use the conventions of scientific reasoning and the norms of documentary production.[11] This program looks like a wildlife documentary, with animal footage, sound bites from scientists, and Voice-of-God narration that presents the "truth" about dinosaurs in their habitat.

Some scholars have wondered how far the link between representation and reality can be stretched without breaking altogether. One researcher explains:

> Given the aggressive use of science fiction in the context of science documentary on cable science channels, the answer may be that it can snap altogether and no one will notice. More problematically, this uncoupling of scientific knowledge and its accurate presentation suggests that the science itself is subjunctive; that is, there is no (scientific) reality outside that which we as a culture believe.[12]

Mr. Peterson ended the lesson by encouraging students to be vigilant about the difference between science fiction, junk science, and science. He showed a video clip from the film, *The Core,* and talked about a recent classroom study, where 70% of college earth-science students incorrectly identified microwaves from the sun as posing a threat to the Earth after watching the film, which features a team of scientists who drill to the center of the Earth and set off a series of nuclear explosions in order to restart the rotation of the Earth's core.[13]

In taking the time to explore the issue of documentary ethics with his students, Mr. Peterson intuitively recognized that this issue is inherently relevant to scientists. Scientists are stakeholders in maintaining a meaningful connection between representation and reality. That's why accuracy and transparency matter so much in scientific research. After the discussion, Mr. Peterson decided that for these science documentaries, they would reflect the core scientific values of accuracy and transparency. As a result, students were discouraged from using fake footage. "It was an executive decision on my part," explained Mr. Peterson, "but kids respected it because we had worked through the process together." This example showcases the responsible use of teacher authority in student media production practice.

Five Challenges in Developing Student Voice Through Media Composition

While few can contest the inherent educational value of student expression, it turns out the reality of media composition can sometimes be way more complicated than the rhetoric. A lot of educators have

worked hard to find ways to include student voice in secondary education, through curriculum design, technology integration, and school
leadership. And there are many eloquent and important arguments
about the necessity of student voice and the prospects of achieving it in
the context of American public education.

But middle-school and high school educators who focus on student expression using media analysis and composition have discovered that there are real challenges to consider. These fascinating
tensions and paradoxes are sometimes underreported both by advocates and by scholars who aren't in the trenches on a daily basis. Here
are a few of the challenges that complicate the real-world practice of
developing youth voice through media composition. At the end of the
chapter, I offer some practical solutions to address these challenges.

Challenge #1: Students Reproduce
Mass Media and Pop Culture Texts

When my son Roger was in high school, he shared a piece of his own
crime fiction writing with a peer. Roger is a writer of detective fiction and
a fan of crime novelist Robert Crais, author of *The Watchman* and *The First
Rule,* which are dark and cinematically written melodramas featuring
flashbacks, dream imagery, and shoot-out climaxes with heavy firepower.

His friend talked about Roger's writing with a school counselor,
who then became concerned. She decided that Roger's writing
needed a review by the school psychologist. His intense, vividly written scenes included knife fights and car crashes, adhering to the codes
and conventions of the crime fiction genre. Naturally, this created
some anxiety among educators operating in the post-Columbine (and
now post-Virginia Tech) atmosphere of anxiety.

Writing and art teachers experience this problem frequently
because they invite students to reveal their hearts, minds, and imagi-
nations. As a result, students often depict scenes of darkness, evil,
violence, or self-harm. As one writer put it, "The students may be
paying homage to their favorite movies or mimicking the world
around them," but teachers wonder how to distinguish between such
imitation and more genuine self-expression.[14] Some part of this process is likely to be developmental, as art teachers tell us that imitation
is the first phase in the process of developing skills. Imitation can
build learners' confidence in using the tools of language, image,
sound, and interactivity in their own creative work.

In student video production activities, impromptu imitation,
performance, and play in front of the camera may lead to clowning,

mock fighting, enacting gender or racial stereotypes, and other forms of transgression, including potentially dangerous behavior, like making chemical explosions, filming from rooftops, or using prop guns.[15] Online, we see a large number of examples of videos made by adolescents who have imitated scenes from movies like *The Fight Club* and MTV shows like *Jersey Shore, Jackass,* and *Silent Library.* Students may face real physical, social, and emotional risks when their media production projects include these types of experiences.

Other risks occur when students reproduce gender or racial stereotypes. When British high school students made a fake magazine called *Slutmopolitan,* it was a complicated mix of sensationalism that was just edgy and ambiguous enough to make the teacher wonder if students were offering a parody or creating a celebration of the explicit sexual content found in women's magazines. When teen girls created a photostory called *The Chippendales,* about a group of white girls who raise money to encourage a group of black boys in the school to undress, the project created an opportunity for students to playfully act out their fantasies. Whether we like it or not, when students have the freedom to develop their voice, they are likely to create distinctly transgressive and carnivalesque messages and themes.[16]

Needless to say, this is not the kind of work that a high school teacher can comfortably show off on the school website. David Buckingham and Julian Sefton-Green note that some academics might interpret these examples as students offering a "critical" perspective on contemporary culture, lapsing "into a kind of romantic celebration which discovers elements of 'resistance'"—but that students themselves might not see their work as critical at all.[17] Educators "must resist the temptation to glamorize student voices, and recognize that the multiple voices that students bring to the classroom, while potentially possessing some elements of resistance and transformation, are likely to be imbued with status quo values."[18]

Challenge #2: Students Challenge Adult Authority

When adolescents have communicative power, it is inevitable that they will say something that makes adults uncomfortable. Adolescents play an important function in society: They are quick to recognize and point out hypocrisy. They notice with disdain the disconnect between adults' ideals and our actions. Fundamentally, this is healthy and important, and it's rooted in their natural idealism.

That's why adolescents have always been part of any genuine process of political, social, or cultural change.

Adults often become uneasy when teens want to talk about their life experiences, especially of matters concerning sexuality and alcohol or drug use.[19] We are often in denial about the role of these experiences in the lives of teens and fear that frank talk validates and normalizes them. Of course, some teens also are learning how to get attention by dressing or acting unusually or by being outrageous or disruptive. Some aspects of media culture reinforce and valorize this behavior, including both the on-screen and off-screen performances of celebrities, athletes, and musicians.

As a result, adults may intentionally close their ears and eyes and use institutional power to silence students whose talk and behavior may offend. In 1988, the Supreme Court ruled that high school students have less First Amendment protection when they speak in curricular settings like a school newspaper, literary magazine, or video production class. School officials "do not offend the First Amendment by exercising editorial control over . . . student speech in school-sponsored expressive activities so long as their actions are reasonably related to legitimate pedagogical concerns."[20] Since the ruling, judges have used Hazelwood v. Kuhlmeier to limit a wide variety of student expression, not just student videos, student-government speeches, and other traditional forms of expression.

A teacher who genuinely wants to support student voice may be at risk of being reprimanded or fired if his or her supervisor finds that students' self-expression may harm the school's reputation or have other negative effects.

Such controversies are truly inevitable. Some of it results from the inappropriate (or shall we say, adolescent) release of bottled-up frustrations, as in the case of an eighth-grade honor roll student at a middle school in the Blue Mountain School District in Pennsylvania, who, after being disciplined for dress code violations, put up a profane and offensive rant on her Myspace page. Without identifying her principal by name, she insinuated that he was a sex addict and pedophile.

Federal judges have upheld the right of school authorities to discipline students or withhold privileges, such as membership in honor societies, for essentially any form of communication or expression that is deemed disruptive, even when created at home and posted on one's personal webpage. As a result, American elementary and secondary students do not have their full First Amendment rights either in school or out of school.

This has important implications for student expression through online media. As noted by the Student Press Law Center, if the emerging precedent "becomes the accepted standard for school disciplinary authority, then the student who criticizes her school superintendent in a letter-to-the-editor can lawfully be punished if readers post profane responses on the newspaper's comment board."[21]

Challenge #3: The Major Production Goes Unfinished

When researcher Lara Beaty observed high school students making videos, working in collaborative teams in urban, suburban, and independent afterschool settings, she documented the uneven practice of video production.[22] Some media projects get started but not completed, often because of a lack of awareness of *how much time* goes into each component in the production process. Projects may also get aborted when plans are too grandiose, when conceptual focus is weak, when there is conflict among team members, or when technical issues interfere with production.

Actually, we know little about the frequency of this problem because there is so much shame associated with it. No educator wants to write about failed lessons and projects, even though if we did, we might be able to offer better ideas about strategies that can be effective in avoiding the types of problems that happen when things go wrong.

Teachers can contribute to student failure: Sometimes they abort student projects when they become too time-consuming. Sometimes teachers' own role in shaping the structure of the project can contribute to failure. When teachers force students to adhere to an elaborate production schedule, an overdrawn-out process can sometimes kill motivation. When students must brainstorm ideas, write scripts, and draw storyboards before they are allowed to touch a camera, they may lose interest in the project before production even starts.

Challenge #4: Coordinating Student Collaboration

In any group project, there can be extreme differentials of effort when it comes to level of involvement. It's just human nature. Some people are leaders, others are somewhat motivated, and still others are just going through the motions. Many students have never worked in collaborative learning groups and need to practice active and tolerant listening, helping one another, giving and receiving constructive criticism, and managing disagreements. That's why teachers must model and reinforce these skills during class.

A major challenge is in the creation of assignments that align with students' skills and abilities and allow for a fair division of time and labor. When one student is assigned to be the video editor, for example, what does this student do for the first weeks of the project when the preproduction and production work is being developed? Creating a full list of production tasks can help groups use a *divide-and-conquer* approach to production, since individual students can be assigned personal responsibility for specific parts of the project.

It's not easy to get small groups of teens to feel a sense of interdependence, where students perceive that they "sink or swim" together. There's an awful lot of nit-picking and in-group/out-group squabbling that is a natural part of how adolescents establish a sense of personal power. However, knowing that peers are relying on you is a powerful motivator for group work.[23]

Challenge #5: Quality of Work Is Superficial When Style Reigns Over Substance

Watch what happens when students create PowerPoint slides as part of their work for an English, history, or health class. In any computer lab in any American high school, students spend a lot of time selecting the design, layout, color, and font style of their projects, but not on the quality of the sentences, ideas, or informational content. This is a bias that results from the unique characteristics of the tool.

That's why teachers are themselves vulnerable to the *style-over-substance* problem. We may be impressed by a student who uses Prezi (www.prezi.com), a zooming presentation editor that animates PowerPoint slides. A student who creates a movie using Xtranormal (www.xtranormal.com) or Animoto (www.animoto.com), an easy-to-use video slideshow tool, may win our praise. Digital tools often privilege visual presentation rather than textual content. For educators, then, this means that we must be especially sensitive to the quality of ideas, the choice of words, and by extension the clarity of argument, in responding to students' media and technology projects.

History educator Daniel Ringrose notes that the general preference for visual rather than textual content also means that student-produced media projects in history may tend to emphasize emotional or dramatic content. Especially in the upper grades, teachers need to be concerned about how the bias of technology composition tools may discourage depth of argument or use of evidence.

When Professor Ringrose asked his students to create multimedia urban history projects, they developed creative approaches to the assignment. But he writes, "Few of our students resisted the temptation to emphasize style over substance, particularly when given tools designed to encourage the former." [24] Multimedia creativity sometimes overwhelms the final product, as students create visually stunning, elegant projects that are empty of meaning. To address this problem, teachers must provide clear guidelines about their expectations for the quality of the argument, message content, and use of evidence. Offering additional time for critique and revision also helps solve the style-over-substance problem.

Challenge #6: Celebrating Completion Leads to an Absence of Reflection or Critique

When students have completed their projects, exhilaration and exhaustion may combine to create a celebratory atmosphere that can discourage the reflective thinking that deepens the quality of the learning experience. Often, the rush to finish a project means there's no time for reflective discussion about either the production process or the completed work itself. When student work is exemplary, culminating celebrations are thrilling and inspirational. But such hoopla can seem empty and superficial when students receive little Oscar awards and applause is showered all around even though productions are not impressive.

It's a shame when there is no time for discussing, after the project has been completed, what aspects of the creative process were more or less effective. When students don't get to examine how actual audience members responded to the work, they miss out on a highly valuable part of the learning experience. Did the audience members' interpretations match our own goals and intentions as authors? That's the challenge we all face in learning to be effective communicators.

Addressing the Challenges of Multimedia Composition in the Classroom

Experienced media teachers know that students may face substantial creative problems that lead their productions to be unimaginative and formulaic. They may face technical problems with lighting, sound, and camera work, which can make videos unwatchable. Unfortunately, those teachers who have experienced a perfect storm of these types of problems may try a production project once and never get the courage to try again! While there's no "quick fix" to the challenges described earlier, overall, students are likely to experience a powerful learning experience when

1. The teacher expresses clarity about the aims and goals of the activity and both teacher and students have adequate levels of comfort with the timetable, production process, and the technology to be used.

2. Students are not just holding the camera or using the software but have a clear sense of agency as "authors" of media messages and make use of the technology tools with intentionality and purpose.

3. The activity includes an appropriate blend of structure and openness about both the process and content, which enables students to demonstrate creativity under constraint.

4. An assessment rubric offers guidance about the value of content over style.

5. The teacher recognizes and uses the "teachable moment" that comes when students face choices that matter, and discussion is used to open up broader questions about the social responsibility of authorship, including values and ethical issues.

6. Opportunities for critique and revision are included so that audiences can share interpretations that enable authors to benefit from *warm feedback* that comments on effective dimensions of student work as well as *cool feedback* that supports reflective thinking and the revision process.

When these challenges are addressed with well-designed assignments and effective instructional practices, multimedia composition projects can deliver on their promise of sustaining students in the process of deep engagement and exploration of ideas.

CHAPTER 5 LESSON PLAN

Periodic Propaganda: A Multimedia Chemistry Project

Welcome to Periodic Industries. You have been hired to sell an individual element. It is your job to research one specific element and tell the world what makes it special and important. To accomplish this, you will create the following:

- *A Poster.* A persuasive poster that visualizes your element's appeal. 30% of grade.
- *A Report.* A two-page written research report on your element about its importance and uses. 40% of grade.
- *A Pitch.* A one-minute persuasive oral presentation to make your audience love your element as much as you do. 30% of total grade.

Research Report Guidelines

In order to persuade people about the worth and value of your element, you must gather information about it. Write a two-page report that includes the following information:

1. Element name, symbol, atomic number, and atomic mass number

2. History of the discovery of the element

3. How the element was named

4. Where the element can be found

5. Common uses of the element

6. Any other interesting trivia you can find that would attract a reader's curiosity

7. A list of works cited, including a minimum of two print and two digital sources, using APA citation format

Poster Guidelines

One of the main assets of the periodic table is how the information is presented: It is very well-structured to represent key ideas. The poster should be created digitally. Use an 8 inch × 8 inch format. Your poster must have these structural elements: (1) Element Name,

(2) Element Symbol, (3) Atomic Number and Mass, (4) Picture, Graphic Art, and (5) Persuasive Slogan or Catchphrase for the Element. The slogan or catchphrase should be a short sentence or statement that will catch the attention and interest of your audience. It can be humorous or serious in tone, but the slogan must communicate something about the element.

Pitch Presentation Guidelines

Speak to audience members to make them feel curious and interested in learning more about your element. Your pitch should present some of the information you learned in the most interesting and accurate way possible. Required elements of the pitch include the following:

1. Display and describe your propaganda poster.

2. Describe key facts about your element, including common uses and where it is found.

3. State your slogan or catchphrase and explain why it's effective.

Developed by Paul Wagenhoffer.

REFLECT

6

Protection and Empowerment

What You'll Find in This Chapter:

- A middle-school health education teacher talks with students about the contradictory messages of celebrity culture, activating prior knowledge, and exploring the lessons that can be drawn from the lifestyles of famous actors, musicians, and athletes.
- Mass media and popular culture provide opportunities for students, parents, and educators to share their interpretations of media messages as filtered through social norms and values.
- Media makers have tried-and-true techniques to attract a large audience, using familiar stereotypes and unexpected contradiction to create juxtaposition that generates surprise and pleasure among audience members.
- Disrupting students' pleasure with advertising and popular culture may activate reactance or be a form of manipulative persuasion. Instead, reflecting on advertising should promote critical autonomy among adolescents.

Lesson Plan:

Positive and Negative Messages in the Media

When Samantha came into Mrs. Jenkins's seventh-grade health class with a low-cut top and her black bra visible, her teacher noticed her right away. How could she not? Samantha's full makeup, including smoky blue eye shadow and red lip gloss, were more than a bit bold for her first period English class. Was this a behavior she should comment on?

Many middle-school teachers experience this ritual of adolescent self-presentation, and it's a topic that's difficult to ignore in the context of ever-changing cultural norms and expectations about fashion, beauty, and gender identity. Once upon a time, the controversy was skirt length or baseball caps or T-shirts with ambiguous slogans; now it's the number of inches of cleavage or abdomen or hip revealed, tattoos and piercings in odd places, or how low a boy's pants ride below the waistline. Dress code issues now concern even educators and parents in the elementary grades. Next year, there will be a new outrageous fashion fad, sure to attract peer attention, creating new must-have items and generating shock and anxiety among parents, teachers, and members of the community.

But as the culture of sexuality keeps reaching down to younger and younger children, parents, teachers, and the general public wonder about media's influence on a young person's sense of personal and social identity. Lawrence Downes describes his experience while attending a middle-school talent show with his daughter, where 11-, 12-, and 13-year-olds writhed and strutted across the auditorium, doing lap dances, grinding, laying on the auditorium floor tilting pelvises, and shaking their chests and bottoms to a Janet Jackson pop song as parents and siblings whistled and applauded.

As Downes put it, "Eroticism in popular culture is a 24-hour, all-you-can-eat buffet," and many children in their early teens are filling up. Adults are generally unreflective about the sexualization of their own children. Kids lose out in this culture of "boy-toy sexuality, where girls' nimble and growing brains are impoverished" without the sense of wider possibilities in life because so much of media culture offers them "a cramped vision of girlhood that enshrines sexual allure as the best or only form of power and esteem."[1]

Superpeers Offer Advice

Researchers don't yet understand exactly why and how young people use media as a type of *superpeer*. That's the term for the function of media characters, celebrities, and athletes as influential figures in the lives of young people. By their behavior, celebrities seem to offer a type of relevant practical advice about various social and personal challenges, just as a slightly older friend or sibling might. Jane Brown at the University of North Carolina at Chapel Hill has found that earlier maturing girls use media personalities this way, having distinctly more interest than later maturing girls in seeing sexual content in movies, television, and magazines, and in listening to sexual content in music, regardless of age or race. Earlier maturing girls are also more likely to be listening to music and reading magazines with sexual content and more likely to see R-rated movies. They are more likely to interpret the messages they see in the media as approving of teens having sexual intercourse.[2]

Similarly, researchers have shown that adolescent girls who read women's magazines are more likely to report being influenced to think about the perfect body, to be dissatisfied with their own body, to want to lose weight, and to diet.[3] So media superpeers shape young teens' perception of what's normal and appropriate when it comes to the process of growing up.

In a report by the American Psychological Association on the sexualization of girls, researchers explained how young teens take their cues from the cultural environment in developing a sense of self. During puberty, both girls and boys begin to evaluate their bodies within the context of their culture. They act and behave in ways that conform both to their local community and to the vast array of media messages that display how teens and young adults should behave, think, and act. For example, many teens may put up pictures of themselves on their Facebook profiles that conform to the visual norms of how they see celebrities, musicians, and athletes depicted every day.

When young people internalize these ideas, it's an effect referred to as *self-objectification*, which involves adopting a perspective of turning one's physical self into an object. People do this when they constantly assess their bodies in an effort to conform to the culture's standards of attractiveness. Girls and young women who are active in the process of self-objectification must work very hard, every day, to meet the salient cultural standard of "sexy." For many young women, it's a time-consuming process, at the very least.

Researchers say that this may lead some girls to evaluate and control their own bodies more in terms of their sexual desirability to others than in terms of their own desires, health, wellness, achievements, or competence.

And this behavior isn't just a matter of putting on makeup or buying tight jeans. In 2010, more than 200,000 teens under age 18 had some kind of cosmetic surgery—including hair removal, nose jobs, and liposuction. In just one year, from 2002 to 2003, the number of girls 18 and younger who got breast implants nearly tripled from

3,872 to 11,326.[4] Television shows like *Extreme Makeover* may contribute to the demand for these services because of the appeal of the before-and-after experience, as we see people cosmetically remade and surrounded by happy friends and family members. Since parental consent for such procedures is required, it's also important to recognize the larger cultural context where parents and other adults support behaviors that are depicted glamorously via the mass media.

Celebrities in the Classroom: Exploring Risk-Taking and Responsibility

After Samantha's sartorial transformation, Mrs. Jenkins watched the film, *Going on 13,* a documentary by Kristy Guevara-Flanagan and Dawn Valadez about four girls growing up in California's East Bay (www .goingon13.com). The film's depiction of four years in the lives of a diverse group of girls from age 10 to 13 was moving. In recalling her own middle-school years, the confusion of puberty came flooding back to her. Mrs. Jenkins remembered the celebrities and musicians that she relied on for a sense of possibility about a life different from her parents. Inspired by the film and her own reflection and reading about media and adolescent identity, Mrs. Jenkins decided to not call out Samantha and comment on her changed appearance. That would just be embarrassing to the girl.

Instead, she introduced a comparison–contrast activity in her health class to encourage all her students to examine their own sense of connectedness to various media personalities and reflect upon the contradictory messages about gender, race, and identity offered up by the mass media and celebrity culture.

She introduced the activity by displaying a couple of examples, putting up side-by-side images of Demi Lovato and Taylor Swift, and asking the following questions: "Who are these people? What do you know about them? How are they similar and how are they different?"

Students knew much more about these celebrities than Mrs. Jenkins did. They knew that Demi Lovato was in rehab. They knew Taylor Swift started her musical career at age 11. Once they got started, Mrs. Jenkins found herself not fully understanding what children were saying. She had to ask *clarifying questions* of the students to elicit more details and context in order to fully understand the ideas and information they were sharing. As she asked these questions, more and more hands were in the air. Students were clearly energized by the process of sharing their knowledge.

Students described two very different visions of young adulthood presented by these celebrities: You could be a nice girl like Anne

Hathaway from *The Princess Diaries*, focused on looking good at all times, saying the right things, and wearing just the right clothes, or you could be a bad girl like Lindsay Lohan, hanging out with the wrong people, taking risks, getting into trouble, and giving people plenty to talk about.

As a means to promote reflection, Mrs. Jenkins asked, "Are these two options a realistic way to think about the process of moving into young adulthood?" Heads nodded solemnly. Kids looked thoughtful. Perhaps it seems that way when you're in the seventh grade. Or maybe there were more than two options. The images of celebrity in contemporary culture offer young people contradictory messages about the costs and benefits of risk-taking and responsibility.

Mrs. Jenkins then displayed images of the African American pop music celebrities Jamie Foxx and Chris Brown, expecting that her African American and Hispanic boys would be more tuned in to these celebrities—and that they'd have a lot to share when she asked them to describe the contradictory messages that celebrities convey by their performances, appearance, and behavior.

"Actually, it was a little unnerving," she remembers when describing the class session. "Students had so much to say." Intense classroom management issues can arise when educators encourage young people to share their knowledge about mass media and popular culture. Mrs. Jenkins admitted that it was not generally like that when discussing seventh-grade health topics like alcohol use or peer pressure. "They're not used to sharing what they know about media in a school context. I was surprised at how deep and complicated their feelings are about these people."

It was challenging for Mrs. Jenkins not to betray her shock at the very serious sense of engagement and connectedness her seventh-grade students were revealing. They clearly wanted to have discussions about the ethical and social responsibilities of being a celebrity. And they wanted to express their opinions about the often complicated and problematic behavior and actions of celebrities.

She was pleased and surprised to see that boys and girls were really listening to each other and responding to each others' ideas. But the conversation got heated at times. Students also challenged others' interpretations. One student got visibly angry when another student made a stupid, gender-stereotyped remark. When Mrs. Jenkins asked students to elaborate on their ideas, some children could offer evidence to support their reasoning. But others were not comfortable sharing the reasoning behind their feelings.

Still, hands were in the air. No heads were on desks. Spontaneous conversations erupted between students in response to certain ideas.

Kids had wildly different feelings about these celebrities, and in the context of expressing themselves, they mentioned many other celebrity names that were unfamiliar to Mrs. Jenkins. She had to insist that students raise their hands before sharing ideas because everyone wanted to talk at the same time. In reflecting on the experience, Mrs. Jenkins said, "It wasn't easy—I'm not used to that much engagement. But it was fascinating and I learned a lot about my kids."

Mrs. Jenkins remembered an article she read in a professional magazine about linking health education and student writing. She wanted her students to use writing as a powerful forum for personal reflection and self-expression. Researchers have shown that students who write about topics they choose freely write lengthier essays and their work is more detailed and clearly organized. Similarly, students who write about topics relevant to their personal and social lives also demonstrate more reflective and more analytical writing.[5]

She combined the Venn diagram activity with a pair-share conversation, culminating in a structured essay-writing activity. Figure 6.1 shows an example of student-produced work.

Next year, Mrs. Jenkins plans to add a role-playing component to this lesson, asking students to create an extemporaneous dramatic presentation that features the positive and negative consequences of risk-taking and responsibility in celebrity culture. "They're at an age where they're dealing with these issues in their everyday lives," she explained.

Figure 6.1 Venn Diagram: Compare and Contrast President Obama and Tiger Woods

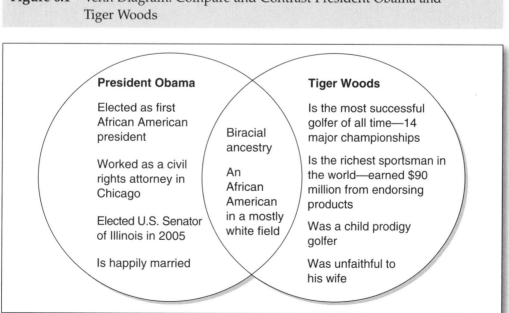

President Obama

Elected as first African American president

Worked as a civil rights attorney in Chicago

Elected U.S. Senator of Illinois in 2005

Is happily married

Biracial ancestry

An African American in a mostly white field

Tiger Woods

Is the most successful golfer of all time—14 major championships

Is the richest sportsman in the world—earned $90 million from endorsing products

Was a child prodigy golfer

Was unfaithful to his wife

Contradictory Messages About Risk and Responsibility

Activity: Use a Venn diagram to illustrate similarities and differences between two celebrities to illustrate how their lifestyle choices reflect ideas about risk and responsibility. Then compose a five-sentence paragraph that summarizes key ideas.

Process

1. Select two famous people from popular culture (including public figures, celebrities, musicians, or athletes) to illustrate some of the contradictory messages about risk and responsibility that are evident in their lifestyle choices.

2. Use library and Internet research tools to gather information about appearance, talent, personal background, and values.

3. Create a Venn diagram to illustrate key similarities and differences between the two individuals.

4. Using the ideas developed through the comparison-contrast activity, compose a five-sentence paragraph describing key ideas.

Criteria for Evaluation

- The paragraph has an attention-getting opening sentence that includes a thesis statement.
- Specific information in the body of the paragraph is used to illustrate both similarities and differences between celebrities.
- The examples showcase specific ideas about celebrity risk-taking and responsibility.
- The writer's point of view about the two figures is evident throughout the essay.
- At least two sources of information are used and sources are correctly cited.

Moral Compass Versus Moral Panic

Some critics and culture watchers call our attention to the problematic messages about gender and race that are used in movies, advertising, and video games. For example, Amy Jussel of Shaping Youth (www.shapingyouth.org) keeps an eagle eye out for all manner of problematic content that may influence children and young people. She has written about Target ads where the big red and white company logo seems to be targeting the genital area of young women; those Carl's Junior hamburger ads featuring bikini models with the slogan, "More Than Just a Piece of Meat"; and Kmart ads that turn the first day of school into a showcase of mean girl stereotypes.

This kind of heads-up on some of the disturbing aspects of contemporary culture is important because it helps adults understand what teens are seeing in the media that we're not. Thanks to Amy Jussel's attention to this issue, I learned about the outdoor ads for a grotesque torture film produced in 2007 by Lionsgate called *Captivity*, which featured four panels showing the following words: "Abduction," with an image of a terrified young blond woman being kidnapped; "confinement," where she's behind a chain-link fence; "torture," in which she is flat on her back, her face in a white cast, with red tubes that resemble jumper cables running into her nostrils; and "termination," where we see her head dangling over the edge of a table, a victim of murder.[6]

It's hard to fathom the audacity of designing outdoor advertising— which can be seen by anyone in a public place—with this level of depravity. *Los Angeles Times* writer Steve Lopez said, "I needed to take a shower just from having been within a hundred feet of it." A young teen he interviewed explained how the image gets "burned into your brain" and stays with you because it's so horrific and shocking. With 30 billboards in Los Angeles and more than 1,400 taxi-top ads, lots of people—including young children—saw these ads before public outrage and pressure forced Lionsgate to remove them.[7]

Some people diminish and trivialize any effort to comment on the disturbing and morally questionable dimensions of media content, identifying this practice as a form of *moral panic*. Some scholars and critics are skeptical about the myth of childhood innocence that is perpetuated by people who try to limit children's access to problematic media content. Some dismiss parents' and educators' concerns about the transgressive aspects of media culture that conflate sexuality, violence, and criminality.

Concerns about misogyny in hip-hop music, violent video games, cyberbullying, sexting, and easy access to pornography are trivialized with the argument that such "public anxiety about the moral regulation of society tends to occur during times of social crisis and particular historical conjunctures," as a response to the novelty of new technologies or as cyclical responses to generational differences.[8] Grass-roots activists concerned about kids' access to porn are stigmatized as being middle-class moralizers as their critics claim that children's exposure to Internet pornography is wildly exaggerated.

In the United States, our First Amendment tradition means that the government has little authority to regulate objectionable media content. That's why we've had very little success with regulatory approaches like the *family hour* (a form of self-regulation where networks limited racy programs to after 9 p.m.) and the *V-chip* (which enables parents to block shows with violence, sexuality, or objectionable language). As a result, it becomes the job of parents to choose whether or not (or how) to attempt to restrict access to particular media content. With wireless broadband in the home, working parents, and a 500-plus channel universe along with the day-to-day visibility of outdoor advertising for torture porn and other kinds of problematic content, most parents feel pretty helpless in this regard.

As a parent, I am a proud protectionist. The parent role is to guide children through life in ways that help them best develop as sensitive, caring, fully human beings. It is not an easy thing to do. But I know that I have been personally influenced by the TV shows, films, books, and images that I've experienced in both positive and negative ways. And I know my kids are similarly influenced by what they read, watch, play, and listen to. My husband and I were aware that our own use of media and technology was the means by which we modeled responsible viewing, listening, and computing. We tried hard not to multitask: When we watched television or movies, that was the primary activity. When we listened to music, we listened. We rarely had the TV on as background noise to life. When we saw troubling news on CNN or heard it on the radio, we shared our emotional responses with our children and told them about our feelings. Even when we were shaken to the core, as on September 11, 2001, we talked about how our hearts were broken by the tragic, poignant personal stories of the victims and their families. We talked about the need to empathize with the people who were experiencing loss and to honor those who made efforts to help. We talked about how media messages about the disaster and its aftermath of two wars were shaping our own sense of national identity and the fresh fears we had as adults about how people around the world perceived our country, the world's largest superpower. As our children entered their teenage years, they could choose their own movies to watch, and we encouraged them to explain to us what they liked about their choices.

Some parents may choose not to limit their children's access to mass media, popular culture, and digital media. These parents hold a view of their children as capable and well able to manage the sometimes challenging, ugly, and difficult aspects of their environment. They see exposure to problematic media content as just one of the many life challenges that are inherent to the process of growing up.

This perspective needs to be recognized and honored. It does no good at all to view parents with these types of attitudes as flawed, irresponsible, or bad parents who need to be fixed.

But whether we like it or not, media messages shape people's beliefs, attitudes, and values. When students, parents, and educators share their opinions and ideas about media content (in the family, in the neighborhood, and more broadly), they express their values and norms.

However, the critics have got one thing quite right: When parents and teachers stand on a soapbox and bemoan the problems of media culture, that's not an effective form of education. It most certainly is *not* the way to develop critical thinking skills. But unfortunately, lecturing like this is a pretty common instructional approach. Parents do it all the time, and it just breeds shame and guilt. Even some college-level media courses adopt an essentially persuasive stance, offering students a slickly produced video with an argument about the dangers of media ownership, sexism in the media, or media violence, without providing the opportunity to engage in the ideas through genuine dialogue, reasoning, or careful, critical examination of evidence.

Cultural critics like Amy Jussel offer a moral compass to a media industry whose relentless pursuit of profit leads it astray. This work serves a powerful educational function for citizens, too. This kind of reflective, public commentary and advocacy about films, video games, and other media is essential in liberal democracies where mass media are controlled by commercial companies and government has little power to control the content of messages. In the United States, such cultural criticism is a truly meaningful strategy that citizens can deploy to get the attention of the general public and mobilize advocacy that gets noticed by government, Hollywood, Silicon Valley, and Madison Avenue.

Celebrities can play a role in establishing the value and visibility of the moral compass. Actress Geena Davis has created a nonprofit organization that focuses on getting more females and more varied portrayals of both female and male characters into movies, TV, and other media aimed at kids 11 and under. That's because content analysis of the representation of female characters has shown that most are highly stereotyped and/or hypersexualized. For example, female characters in G-rated films wear virtually the same amount of sexually revealing clothing as female characters in R-rated films.[9]

Joss Whedon, famous for his TV show *Buffy the Vampire Slayer*, spoke out about the depravity behind the crass marketing effort in *Captivity* and the more general tendency to depict the torture or abuse of women as a form of spectacle. He writes, "Women's inferiority—in fact, their malevolence—is as ingrained in American popular culture as it is anywhere they're sporting burkhas. I find it in movies, I hear it in the jokes of colleagues, I see it plastered on billboards, and not just the ones for horror movies. Women are weak. Women are manipulative. Women are somehow morally unfinished. And the logical extension of this line of thinking is that women are, at the very least, expendable." Whedon invites his fans to take action, "because it's no longer enough to be a decent person. It's no longer enough to shake our heads and make concerned grimaces at the news. True enlightened activism is the only thing that can save humanity from itself. "[10]

The Casting Agent: Your Life as a Movie

Reflect and Write: Whom would you cast to play you in a movie version of your life? Who should play the part of your close family members and friends? Would you base the decision on appearance alone, or also on personality, mannerisms, and other factors? What key parts of your story or your personality would you want to be captured accurately? What aspects could be fictionalized?

Source: The *New York Times* Learning Network.

Understanding Stereotypical and Contradictory Messages in Popular Culture

Why do media producers present contradictory messages? Media makers are not the enemy. Their job is to create stories that compel our attention, because attention is the commodity that has value in the marketplace. Media makers and distributors get money from advertisers, and in exchange, provide them with access to eyeballs. Some people think that media companies (like TV networks, radio stations, magazines, websites, or Internet service providers) simply sell radio or TV time, online banner ads, or space in a print publication. But this is inaccurate. Media companies are in the business of selling human attention, and it's sold in units by the thousand, depending on the age, income, race, geographic region, and other characteristics of the audience.

Audiences pay for media products directly and indirectly. We pay directly when we pay our newspaper, magazine, cable, or telecommunications bill. At the same time, we also pay indirectly through the purchase of goods and services. Some of the money we pay for products and services including food, transportation, clothing, and almost everything else goes to support various types of advertising that subsidize the distribution of information and entertainment. Some estimates suggest that between 10% and 40% of the cost of goods and services ends up supporting the distribution of information or entertainment through company marketing, public relations, and advertising. For example, in 2006, American businesses spent $265 billion on media. One company, Proctor & Gamble, spends $3 billion each year to get people's attention to persuade them to buy consumer goods. This economic model is sometimes called the *dual revenue stream* because media distributors get money from two sources: advertisers and audiences. This economic model of paying for information and entertainment has some strengths and weaknesses. Depending on whether you're looking from the point of view of the audience, the advertiser, the media distributor, or the author, you might see the pros and cons differently.

When we watch reality TV shows, the stories that grab our attention are the ones full of both stereotype and contradiction: the charming and handsome bachelor who displays his deceitfulness freely through backbiting and mean-spirited talk, or on TV news, when we see the generous and loving father, who just bought his teen daughter a new sports car. Now fallen upon hard times after losing his job, he's in the news for murdering his wife before killing himself.

Readers, viewers, and listeners pay attention to stereotypes because they are *familiar*. We pay attention to contradiction because it's novel and *unexpected*.

Media producers are more interested in generating surprise and pleasure than in maintaining coherence or consistency. Seeking to attract the attention of the largest possible audience, producers create or develop ideas that use familiar tropes but also stand out from the clutter. The contradictory messages we receive from mass media do attract our attention—but, ironically, contradiction and stereotypes in mass media and popular culture are sometimes so ubiquitous that we don't notice it.

What is the impact of contradictory messages? Does mass media's use of contradiction and juxtaposition create a surrealistic frame that abandons logic, reason, and sequence? If so, such juxtaposition may promote a *spectator mentality* toward social and political knowledge, where we can watch injustice and degradation on the many screens in our lives but feel no need to take these messages seriously or respond to them sanely.

On the positive side, however, multiple, contradictory messages also may contribute to the perception that the world is an open realm of possibilities. As David Gauntlett points out, "We no longer get singular, straightforward messages about ideal types of male and female identities (although certain groups of features are clearly promoted as more desirable than others). Instead, popular culture offers a range of stars, icons and characters from whom we can acceptably borrow bits and pieces of their public persona for use in our own."[11]

But when I think about how our culture's focus on physical and verbal aggression has become a staple of entertainment culture, it bothers me. Everywhere we see *playful power* as a vital part of entertainment culture. Physical and relational aggression, which peaks during the middle-school years, happens when friendships are used as a weapon of sorts. We see mean girls and players everywhere on television and in the movies. Young men and women may tend to evaluate their own lives and their own social relationships in terms of the sheer entertainment value, treating friends as dramatic objects to be used or abused for one's own amusement. Because mass media have made *relational aggression* a normal, everyday part of our storytelling culture, it's not surprising to find young teens trying out some of the ploys they see in the movies (and inventing their own).

Advertising, Identity, and Pleasure

There's no separating entertainment, advertising, and education. Thanks to product placement, teen girls who watch the movie *Mean Girls* will see products for Coca-Cola, Red Bull, Cheetos, and Doritos, as well as fashion items from Burberry and Louis Vuitton. Psychologically, viewers are invited to make an emotional connection between our consumption of these products and the feelings we experience watching characters on the screen.

Ads are a highly familiar part of our cultural environment. Familiarity breeds liking. There's a kind of pleasure that we experience when familiar brands and products show up in popular media. Teens have pleasurable associations about the many different brands in their lives. The average 10-year-old has memorized the names of 300–400 brands. Teens ages 12–19 spent more than $170 billion in purchases in 2002 for food and beverages, video and digital media, apparel, and health and beauty care.[12] Online, young people get text message advertising on their cell phones and play video games where branded products are showcased as part of the digital environment. Consumer culture offers teens a shared repository of images, characters, plots, and themes that serve as the basis for social interaction and play.

Advertising's blending of fantasy and reality offers a little jolt of stimulation and a sometimes pleasurable escape from the routines of our everyday and often mundane lifestyles. Advertising reflects and reinforces a truly American cultural value: All our needs and desires can be gratified by a purchase of some kind.

Have Americans Been Programmed to Shop?

Activity: Students stage a videotaped debate about Americans, advertising, and shopping and then select compelling sound bites from their performance to capture key ideas.

Background. In a 2008 *New York Times* article, Peter Goodman writes, "For decades, Americans have been effectively programmed to shop. China, Japan and other foreign powers have provided the wherewithal to purchase their goods by buying staggering quantities of American debt. Financial institutions have scattered credit card offers as if they were takeout menus and turned our houses into A.T.M.'s. Hollywood and Madison Avenue have excelled at persuading us that the holiday season is a time to spend lavishly or risk being found insufficiently appreciative of our loved ones."

Process. Working in small groups, students stage a debate on the question: Are Americans effectively programmed to shop?

Assign one small group to take the "pro" position and the other group to take the "con" position. Each side should take three minutes to make its argument.

Videotape the debates and post the raw footage online. For homework, ask students to review the video and select the five best sound bites that capture the most compelling ideas, pro or con. *Sound bites* are brief statements, taken from a longer piece of speech, that capture key ideas in a catchy, memorable way.

Finally, *review and discuss* the choices students made and use discussion to generate a list of why sound bites are so effective in the communication process.

Reactance and Resistance

New forms of advertising are everywhere online. There are banner ads on websites, ads that run before you view a video, and pop-up ads that display under the video. To give viewers a feeling of control, some websites let users choose among ads that are presented before the content. Some YouTube videos are forms of advertising, too. Of course, there also are promotional trailers from companies like Viacom and Time Warner. But there's also a lot of advertising that doesn't look like advertising. One popular online video showed people sitting around a table, holding their cell phones close to a few unpopped popcorn kernels. When the phones ring in unison, the kernels of popcorn pop! When it was revealed that this video was created by a technology company to sell wireless headphones, consumers were able to understand how online videos can be used in *stealth marketing* campaigns. Funny amateur videos turn out to have been produced to sell Gatorade, Levi's, and Nike. Viewers are punked by stealth marketing when they interpret these messages as simple entertainment and are unaware of their persuasive intent.[13]

Some educators attempt to disrupt students' pleasure with advertising and media culture by demonstrating how advertising promotes "a sense of inadequacy, anxiety, shame, yearning, envy and contempt for the self or the other."[14] Because the values of consumer culture are so deeply woven into the fabric of our society, providing students with a disruptive, alternative interpretation of advertising may create a shock to the system that moves students toward critical distance.

That's why some teachers use instructional approaches borrowed from anticorporate activism to expose the exploitive practices of consumer culture and thereby produce *reactance*, the psychological response that occurs when people get angry when they feel they are being manipulated.

One approach, called critical media literacy, emphasizes "the politics of representation . . . of gender, race, class and sexuality," by bringing a focus on ideology, power, and domination.[15] Here the goal is to activate resistance to media culture by demonstrating how the media's corporate agenda is to make profit. Of course, companies like Disney and Viacom make their profit goals highly transparent. Every decision made by these media companies is filtered through the lens of cost and benefit, income and expenses.

When this approach translates into work with middle-school and high school students, there's a tendency for teachers to vilify media industries for their profit-seeing motives in attracting large audiences. In one curriculum, titled *Healthy Within Girl Talk*, students look at magazine covers, analyzing the images presented on the covers and commenting on what they imply about women and men. The curriculum states, "Take a class vote—is this ad positive or negative? If they vote that it is negative, have one of the group members crumple up the ad and toss it on the floor. Tell them this is symbolic of throwing out all of the negative feelings that ad makes us feel." In another lesson, titled "Media Action," students are shown two posters: One has images of different people of all races, ages, and shapes, while the other has pictures of the same person over and over. Students are asked to comment on the posters and respond to the prompt, "Which is a world you'd rather live in?"[16]

Try to imagine the level of student dialogue that this prompt question would generate. How many students would respond in earnest? How many would offer smarmy, smart-alecky responses? Might some high school students feel coerced and manipulated by the tone and sentiment of this lesson?

Not only must we question whether this approach actually activates genuine critical thinking skills, we must consider the possibility that the presentation of gender stereotypes in the classroom may have a backfire effect—and actually activate and reinforce gender stereotypes instead of challenging them. When using images of stereotyped depictions of ethnic stereotypes, some researchers have found that media literacy videos may increase prejudicial responses, even when the goal of the video is to diminish such feelings.[17]

When students are invited to identify the restricted portrayals of females, noticing their positioning as passive victims, and counting the prominence of romance and fashion themes, they don't always come to the same conclusions as their teachers. And when students don't necessarily value this type of learning experience, well-meaning teachers are often surprised. As researchers Jane Kenway and Elizabeth Bullen explain, "The students do not tend to appreciate teachers who make them feel ashamed about their choices and lifestyles—all in the name of helping them. Indeed, a number of them find this insulting and hurtful."[18]

When teachers choose to deconstruct media messages that students consider to be pleasurable, there can be an emotional fallout. David Buckingham warns us about how researchers may oversimplify "the complex and messy realities of classroom practice. Especially when it comes to the areas with which media education is so centrally concerned (e.g., with what students see as their own culture and their own pleasures), they may well be inclined to resist or reject what teachers tell them."[19]

That's why the concept of *critical autonomy* is an essential component of digital and media literacy education. This concept was first articulated by British educator Len Masterman, who argued that the key task of media teachers is to "develop in pupils enough self-confidence and critical maturity to be able to apply critical judgments to media texts which they will encounter in the future."[20] To support the development of critical autonomy, teaching and learning must be student-centered and inquiry-oriented. It focuses not on transmitting knowledge but on meaning-making and a respect for diverse interpretations.

For genuine reflection to occur, every idea and argument must be placed under the microscope for critical scrutiny. It's not about getting kids to think like the teacher or share the teacher's worldview. There's nothing persuasive or coercive about digital and media literacy education—except in one regard: We valorize the importance of questioning assumptions, asking questions, and reflecting on one's own processes of interpretation.

CHAPTER 6 LESSON PLAN

Positive and Negative Messages in the Media

Overview: Students create a chart of the positive and negative messages about health, lifestyles, and relationships contained in a sample of familiar television programming.

Time: One class period

Learning Outcomes:

- Actively interpret media messages using prior knowledge, values, and attitudes.
- Clarify ideas through participating in both a large-group and small-group discussion experience.
- Evaluate the role of media as a source of both entertainment and information.
- Recognize how meanings are communicated visually and through narrative storytelling.
- Reflect on how media messages can affect decision making about health and relationships.

Introducing the Lesson

Students will be learning new ways to "read" television programs, music, movies, and media. And they'll get a chance to "write" by composing a media message, too. Digital and mass media can (and should) be studied systematically just as we do with print media.

Activity: Make a list of your five favorite television programs, the shows you try not to miss each week. Ask this: What do you like best about these programs? Encourage a diverse array of responses and make sure that students show respect in listening to others' ideas. This is essential in helping foster productive discussion among middle-school students.

Positive Messages in the Media

Explain: Television programs often feature characters and storylines that depict the most positive aspects of human behavior. You may define positive messages using concepts from character education, messages that depict friendship, loyalty, courage, respect, and compassion. You might describe a TV program that you especially enjoy watching and explain some of the positive messages of the show.

Ask this: What are some of the positive messages that are presented in your favorite shows? Encourage a variety of responses.

Negative Messages in the Media

Explain: Television shows provide a complex mix of both positive and negative messages regarding the challenges of life. You might give an example of a negative message from a TV show you've seen. Negative messages show the worst aspects of human behavior. You may want to define negative messages using the model of the seven deadly sins: greed, lust, envy, pride, anger, sloth (laziness), and gluttony (overeating). Ask this: What are some of the negative messages that are presented in your favorite shows?

Collaborate

Students work in small groups of two or three to fill in details of some positive and negative examples from TV shows using the worksheet titled, "Positive and Negative Messages in the Media" (see p. 122). When they have completed the chart, invite each small group to share their best example of how a television program depicts positive and negative messages.

Explain: Sometimes a specific character, behavior, or visual depiction can be simultaneously positive and negative, and some may be hard to classify. It's OK if students disagree about whether a specific example is positive or negative—as long as students provide reasoning and evidence to support their ideas.

Conclusion

Sometimes people believe that TV shows are just entertainment. But becoming a critical viewer means recognizing that all messages are educational in some sense. A media literate person learns to distinguish between the many positive and negative messages that are shown in the media. People can learn from both positive and negative messages about our society. Congratulate the class on recognizing the underlying messages that are all part of the TV viewing experience.

Assessment

The quality of student examples in the completed worksheet should demonstrate an understanding of how both healthy and unhealthy behaviors are depicted in entertainment TV programming.

Source: "The Media Straight Up!" Media Literacy Curriculum, Drug Free Pennsylvania (www.medialiteracyguide.org).

WORKSHEET

Positive and Negative Messages in the Media

NAME: _____

INSTRUCTIONS: Working with a partner, write down some examples of positive and negative messages that you have encountered on your favorite TV shows. Describe a specific example in the space provided.

	POSITIVE Messages About People, Healthy Behaviors, and Relationships	NEGATIVE Messages About People, Healthy Behaviors, and Relationships
NAME OF TV SHOW		
Example		
Example		
NAME OF TV SHOW		
Example		
Example		

A full-sized reproducible of this worksheet can be found at www.corwin.com/medialiteracy

7

Life Online

What You'll Find in This Chapter:

- Cultivating digital citizenship can help balance the fine line between students' right to self-expression and the need to keep school a place that's free from disruption.
- Sharing controversial content is appealing to adolescents, who are developmentally tuned in to take risks in pursuit of experience.
- Teachers can open up conversational space to examine ethical and social issues associated with controversial content online.
- When we consider the point of view of the subject, the author, and the audience of social media messages, we can apply ethical reasoning based on Golden Rule values.
- Discussion of the "scary maze game" YouTube videos, which show people playing pranks on each other, can help reflect on issues concerning the relationship between social power and pleasure.

Lesson Plan:

Online Relationships: Conducting an Interview

Educators are well aware that what happens in students' lives outside of the classroom affects them in school. When the football team wins a big game, the pride and energy can expand and energize teenagers' heads and hearts and make the whole building a happy place. When there's gossip brewing in the cafeteria, the negative energy can spill into the hallways and classrooms. When a popular student faces a major health crisis, students' fears and anxieties can be palpably felt as they notice the missing kid and the empty desk. When students aren't sleeping enough at home, we see them yawning, propping their heads up, and fading away in class before our very eyes. When students' off-campus speech affects their on-campus life, it can disrupt the process of education.

The Internet provides tremendous opportunities for both education and leisure. There's no doubt about the significant value of *participatory culture,* a term used to define the Internet's openness to amateurs and its support of the creative practices of ordinary people.[1] The flowering of DIY ("do it yourself") values that are embedded in many online communities holds tremendous promise for supporting people's social interaction in ways that enrich our culture and support practices of self-governance.

But the Internet also offers some considerable challenges. We live now in a time where social networking software explicitly encourages people to share every quiver and shiver of their lives, where the very words "participation" and "connection" are automatically magical, it seems. As a result, when inappropriate sharing or relational aggression happens on Facebook and Myspace, its impact can reverberate across many aspects of school life.

The most well-publicized, school-related events involve suicides, where students have been humiliated by their friends and suffer mental anguish that results in taking their own lives. These very uncommon events build public awareness about how young people's online lives affect personal and social identity. But even more minor cases also reveal the complexity of drawing the line between students' right to expression and the need to keep a school free from disruption. See the following, for example:

- When one Florida high senior started the Facebook group, "Ms. Teacher Name Is the Worst Teacher I've Ever Met!" she posted a photo of her teacher and an invitation to her peers to express their feelings. Her friends posted comments supporting the teacher and she took the page down after two days.

The student was suspended for three days for disruptive behavior, removed from Advanced Placement classes, and assigned to regular classes.

- In another case, an eighth-grade student created a website titled "Teacher Sux," where the student requested money to "pay for the hitman" and posted other comments so threatening that the algebra teacher was unable to return to teaching. The student was suspended, placed in a special education program for disruptive students, and was not allowed to participate in graduation.

- A student posted an angry message on her blog when she complained about a school activity being cancelled "due to douchebags in central office." In response, the principal prohibited her from running for senior class secretary, claiming her incivility was disruptive to school functioning.

- A middle-school student in Costa Mesa, California, created an online group on Myspace with the title, "I Hate Classmate's Name." There was an expletive, an anti-Semitic reference, and a post that read, "Who here wants to take a shotgun and blast her in the head over a thousand times?" All 20 students who joined the group were suspended.

- In 2005, a high school student at Hickory High School in Hermitage, Pennsylvania, was suspended after he created a parody profile of his principal on Myspace. The student accessed the website during his Spanish class, showed the site to another student, and was then told to shut it down. In the "Tell me about yourself" question, he had written the following: "Birthday: Too drunk to remember. Are you a health freak: Big steroid freak. Ever shoplifted: Big bag of Kmart." The student was suspended.

Of course, students engage in malicious and hurtful online and offline behavior toward their peers even more frequently than they rage against their teachers. That's why I have some sympathy for school leaders who are frustrated when they find themselves spending all day addressing problems related to various Facebook disputes involving insults to staff and students. But how should these disputes be handled? As the aforementioned examples show, some forms of discipline seem appropriate. But in some of these cases, the punishment seems extreme.

It's difficult to find a balance between students' right to free expression and school leaders' need to create an environment conducive to learning. The legal landscape seems split as judges decide when online student speech does or does not cause *material disruption.* Principals face a legal minefield when they use suspensions and other penalties in inappropriate ways. Courts have stated clearly that a student "should be free to speak his mind when the school day ends" and that school administrators' disciplinary power must be restricted to the boundaries of the school itself.[2]

To help students acquire the competencies of digital citizenship, we have to do more than make students sign an acceptable use policy statement or post technology usage rules in the computer lab. In addition to celebrating the most exciting ways that digital media support and enhance learning, we have to engage students in frank and authentic conversations about the problematic and challenging kinds of experiences they have online as they create and share messages. At the end of this chapter, you'll find a lesson that supports the development of reflective thinking through the process of interviewing someone about their online relationships.

Digital Citizenship

Students understand human, cultural, and societal issues related to technology and practice legal and ethical behavior. Students

1. advocate and practice safe, legal, and responsible use of information and technology;

2. exhibit a positive attitude toward using technology that supports collaboration, learning, and productivity;

3. demonstrate personal responsibility for lifelong learning; and

4. exhibit leadership for digital citizenship.

Source: The International Society for Technology in Education (ISTE) National Educational Technology Standards (NETS).

Online Communication Habits and Social Power

Lots of people are using social networking tools as a major part of their daily life. Some people communicate online more than they do face-to-face. A survey of social-media-using women ages 18–34 shows that 26% get up in the middle of the night to read text messages and 21% check Facebook during the night. A full 37% of women reported falling asleep with their cell phone in their hands.[3] Zadie Smith tells the story of her own addictive experience with Facebook at work:

> As with all seriously addictive things, giving up proved to be immeasurably harder than starting. I kept changing my mind: Facebook remains the greatest distraction from work I've ever had, and I loved it for that. I think a lot of people love it for that. Some work-avoidance techniques are onerous in themselves and don't make time move especially quickly: smoking, eating, calling people up on the phone. With Facebook hours, afternoons, entire days went by without my noticing.[4]

To really make sense of people's use of online social media, we must understand how social power is implicated. *Social power* is the ability to gratify our own human needs through manipulating the quality of our relationships with various people around us.[5] This is particularly relevant to teens and young people, who are learning about social power through everyday social interaction. Posting and sharing online is a form of that learning. Social power can be bewildering or intoxicating at first; learning to handle it is an important part of growing up.

Depending on your reference group, what counts as social power varies. Teachers may gain social power by posting lesson plans online and getting feedback from their colleagues around the country. Amateur chefs may gain social power by sharing recipes or making online video demonstrations of cooking techniques. Among video game players, posting a new cheat code may help you gain status with people in the gaming community. If you're into fashion and makeup, you may get social power by posting a photo of yourself in a new look.

The Multitasking Mind

Discussion Activity: People often use online social media at the same time they do many other work and leisure activities. Consider the following statements and decide which ones you agree or disagree with. Use evidence and reasoning to support your opinion.

- Multitasking is an essential skill needed to function in the 21st century.
- Multitasking keeps your brain active.
- Multitasking can have a negative effect on relationships because of the lack of focused attention.
- The need to multitask inhibits imagination because there is not enough downtime for daydreaming and reflection.
- Multitasking can result in not doing each task as well as if it were done with a singular focus.

Controversial Online Content

Adolescents are developmentally focused on taking risks, pursuing experience for the sake of experience, and seeking out novelty, complexity, and intense situations. That's how they learn the skills they need to become independent adults.

Many parents and teachers feel like children and young people are the experts when it comes to online media. That's one reason why teachers and parents are unlikely to initiate conversations about controversial online content, in part because of ignorance and in part because of confusion about how to talk about it.

But one out of three teens has seen violent or hateful content online. Most all teens have seen pornographic content.[6] Being exposed to unwanted sexual content or receiving an unwanted sexual solicitation can be traumatic for teens.[7] In one study of European children and youth, it was found that teenagers encounter more online risks than younger children and that boys encounter more exposure to violent and sexual content. In particular, teen boys "appear to pay less attention to online risk, suggesting they may be harder to reach in terms of safety advice—an issue since they encounter more risk." Teenage boys are also most likely to perpetuate risk by bookmarking pornographic or violent online content and sending it to friends.[8]

There are healthy and unhealthy ways to acquire social power. Unfortunately, among some teen boys and young men, one quick and easy way to gain social power is to watch or create a drinking video. There are thousands of them online. Several have more than one million page views. These videos feature young people drinking to excess, sometimes with humiliating consequences.

Offensive content of all kinds is protected by the U.S. Constitution under the First Amendment. (In 2010, the Supreme Court struck down a 1999 law that halted the practice of selling "crush" videos that depicted tiny animals being crushed to death. The law came under challenge when it was used to prosecute a man who sold dogfighting videos.)

More than 90% of American kids ages 8 to 15 have seen online porn, and in fact, the porn industry takes active steps to attract children by "typo-squatting"—buying the domain names of frequently misspelled URLs.[9] At least 26 names of cartoon characters are linked to porn sites, which means that kids searching for their favorite movies and TV shows accidentally stumble upon porn. About one-third of Internet users receive exposure to porn through links disguised under different names.[10]

In addition to porn, controversial online content can be tasteless, gruesome, obscene, emotionally disturbing, full of rage and pain, or just plain bizarre. Videos may feature Holocaust deniers, exhibitionists, and dangerous drivers. You can learn cutting and other forms of self-mutilation by watching online videos. And fight videos are popular online entertainment, which feature children, teenagers, or young adults engaged in real or staged fighting.

> ### Online Videos: What We Like and Dislike
>
> **Discussion Activity:** In a two-minute pair-share activity, students describe examples of online videos they like and dislike. Then on the blackboard, each student writes the name and short phrase describing two videos. Which ones might be considered controversial? What makes them controversial?

In the context of the classroom, do not be tempted to take a look at an online video that a student mentions or describes. It's natural to become curious about a video, especially if it is described well. After talking about them, students will ask to screen videos in class. But remember the developmental characteristics of adolescence—taking risks is normative for teenagers (and for some, punking the teacher is quite a coup). Don't screen a video in a classroom that you haven't previewed first outside of class.

Opening Up Conversational Space

How do parents and teachers open up a respectful and safe conversational space to examine ethical and social issues associated with controversial online content? It's not easy, that's for certain. Lots of teens will shrug off controversial content as no big deal, maintaining a pose of disinterested stoicism to avoid revealing genuine feelings on a complex and controversial topic.

Many teens maintain high levels of secrecy involving their online activities and will not admit to exposure to offensive content or participation in problematic behaviors.[11] Others may say, "It was upsetting" or "I wish I hadn't seen it," but this may be uncomfortable to reveal in front of peers.

Many of the funniest and most popular YouTube videos can be analyzed in terms of the transgressive humor that's used to attract and hold audience attention. As one scholar explains, "Humor in general consists of a play with meaning, openness to the possibility about science, the law, medicine, anthropology, criminal justice, psychiatry, and other fields. Many producers make a substantial effort to get the facts right. When Professor Robert T. Brennan of the Harvard School of Medicine was watching the TV show *Law & Order,* he was stunned to see a character quoting the results of his recently published study on gun violence. Explained Brennan, "It was more accurate than anything I've ever had covered in a newspaper."[5]

When science news and current events are featured on prime-time entertainment, significant, measurable learning can result. For example, some episodes of *ER* featured stories about date rape. Before the show aired, only 10% of viewers were aware that high-dose birth control pills were an option to prevent pregnancy. In the week after the episode aired, 33% of viewers were aware of the morning-after option. Another episode dealt with HPV as a cause of cervical cancer, and before the show ran, 24% of *ER* viewers knew about HPV. A week after the show aired, nearly 50% said they had heard of HPV.[6]

Civic Education Today

Today, politics has become a dirty word. Negative campaigning and partisanship now contribute to increased polarization, apathy, and disengagement on the part of American citizens. As John McManus has explained, increased competition for smaller audiences has led to a rash of cheapening and corner-cutting as cash-strapped news organizations struggle to maintain quality.[7]

While an older generation views citizenship as an obligation, with voting as the core democratic act and becoming well-informed about public issues and government a responsibility, younger people may feel differently. A generational shift in citizenship styles is occurring. Increased mistrust of the media means young people may not believe much of what they hear, see, or read on the news. Many young people are focused on personal, individual expression, not on working collaboratively to make changes in their community. Instead of joining a local political party or running for office, young adults may participate in networks of interest-group communities, based on issues like the environment, jobs, gender equity, democracy in developing nations, or social justice.[8]

For many people, news is shared casually and primarily through word of mouth. People learn about events of the day from *opinion leaders,* a group of peers, friends, and other colleagues who informally share what they've learned from reading or watching the news with those who don't consume news directly.

of a meaningless world, and introduction of disorder. It implies surprise, loss of control, openness to novelty and ambiguity, and disengagement with regard to truth, morality, and affection."[12]

So I wasn't surprised when one high school student told me about *Fred,* a series of YouTube videos created by Lucas Cruikshank. In these videos, he is a fast-talking, working-class teenager pretending to be a little kid by jumping on beds and having temper tantrums.[13]

Students recognize that the *Fred* videos were simultaneously funny and a little bit controversial. One student explained, "They feature this kid, and he's acting like a baby and he has a distorted voice. He lives with his mother who is drug-addicted and alcoholic." One episode implied that Fred has been the victim of child abuse (being locked in a dog cage for three days). British researchers Sonia Livingstone and Nancy Thumin explain why these YouTube videos appeal to children and teens: "Over and again, by touching on the taboos of our time— child neglect, poverty, abuse—the viewer is forced to recognize the pathos and powerlessness of children in an intolerant world."[14]

Fred videos also make sense to young people growing up with *South Park* and *Family Guy,* two popular television shows that feature children offering comments about various social taboos. Teens are aware that *Family Guy, South Park,* and online *Fred* videos contradict normative adult ideas about family values. As Stuart Hall explains, such messages are ubiquitous in part because they construct "a symbolic frontier between the 'normal' and the 'deviant,' the 'normal' and the 'pathological,' the 'accepted' and the 'unacceptable,' what 'belongs' and what is 'Other,' between 'insiders' and 'outsiders,' Us and Them."[15]

High school students readily acknowledge the built-in challenges of the culture of secrecy on the online playground. While educators and technology experts around the world may celebrate the positive values of amateur video production, students themselves are well aware of the many YouTube video productions that are simultaneously trivial and problematic, like sex videos, fight videos, or prank videos. To discover how to best discuss problematic content in the context of a classroom interaction at the secondary level, I decided to focus on exploring one particular type of YouTube video: the scary maze game videos.

Scary Maze Game Videos

I have never met a 12- to 19-year-old who isn't familiar with this prank. The video phenomenon began around 2002 when interactive flash videos known as *scare pranks* or *scary mazes* began to emerge across the Internet. Upon clicking the link, the viewer is presented with a puzzle game that requires a high level of concentration, only to be disrupted by an ear-piercing scream and ghastly photos from horror films. Scary maze websites were originally shared via e-mail, chat rooms, or instant messages before the advent of YouTube.

High school students confirm the popularity of these videos. When I asked a group of 10th-grade students how many had played the maze game, all but two hands went up into the air. When I asked how many had seen a YouTube video about the prank, all but three hands were raised. One high school student had even created a scary maze video herself, featuring a family member being pranked.

As of April 2010, a YouTube search on the keywords "scary maze game" displayed 8,620 results, which generally show videos depicting a person who is scared by playing the game. Videos have been created by YouTube users from Spain, France, Germany, Turkey, China, and other countries. The top-ranked video, shown in Figure 7.1, Scary Maze Prank—The Original, has been viewed nearly 20 million times, attracting more than 44,000 comments.

Figure 7.1   Scary Maze Prank—The Original

The video features a young boy playing the maze game on his home computer. When startled by the sound of screaming and a gruesome face dripping with blood, he screams, hits the computer monitor instinctively, and then runs away from the computer, crying uncontrollably in a deeply visceral fear response.

I made the decision to show one of the scary maze game videos in a high school classroom in order to open up a dialogue about our ethical and social responsibilities in sharing online video and other content. I chose one that features a young girl, about age 7, playing the game while seated at a computer. I deliberately darkened the room before screening the video. At the moment of the scare, the child cries and sobs uncontrollably, looking to her mother for comfort as the adults in the room laugh. As is typical for every audience, students spontaneously laughed when watching the child's reaction.

Sharing Emotional Responses

We sat in a semidarkened room during the viewing experience, and during the sharing of reactions, we kept the room dark. I asked students to use this structured verbal response: "This made me feel (fill in the blank) because (fill in the blank)." Students expressed ideas like this:

> "It made me feel happy because it's hilarious to watch the way the kid reacts."

> "It made me feel excited because I knew what was going to happen."

> "It made me feel angry because there is an adult there who is exploiting a child."

This structured verbal format is not necessary for all students to engage in sharing feelings, but I have found that it tends to equalize the differences between students who are more and less comfortable with expressing their feelings. It encourages them to use full sentences while describing and reflecting on their feelings and promotes divergent responses, too. It solves one of the big problems when engaging in discussion with young people: their tendency to repeat the same ideas over and over, even when the point has already been made. A structured discourse form helps students recognize both the more common and the more original and distinctive ideas that emerge as people share their thoughts, feelings, and ideas.

When reviewing the comments posted in response to this particular YouTube video, we see some of the tensions people experience when they encounter both the pleasure and the anxiety of videos that feature young children being scared. Some examples from the YouTube user comments include these statements:

"Lol this is funny."

"The way he cries is sooooo funny."

"Even if it scars him for life it was worth it."

"That is such a mean thing to do to a child."

"Funny to prank on a grown-up; not funny to do to a kid."

"Funny vid yes but u do know u just destroyed ur child's trust."

The Pleasure of the Prank

Pranking videos can serve as a starting point for launching critical conversations about the complex ethical relationships that exist among users of online social media. Nearly everyone knows somebody who takes delight in playing pranks. The pleasure of the prank can be described by the concept of *symbolic inversion,* where expressive behavior inverts or contradicts commonly held cultural codes, values, and norms.[16] By inverting power relationships, pranksters gain a form of social power. One researcher explains as follows: "The greater the distance between the prankster and the fool, whether in age or professional position or perceived social status, the greater the victory for the prankster."[17]

Historically, pranking is well-documented in both ancient and medieval literature. Puns, jokes, and humorous rituals were a typical part of medieval culture. By raising the power of the prankster and lowering the power of the ones fooled, *communities of laughter* maintained patterns of social exclusion or inclusion, reputation or contempt.[18]

Indeed, YouTube pranks are similar to older types of media productions that involve startling or surprising people to document their reactions. For example, some television viewers of the 1950s and 1960s remember *Candid Camera,* a program that featured ordinary people being pranked by small crises and other unexpected events that host Allen Funt noted could occasionally veer into the realm of cruelty. Funt once explained to an interviewer, "If you want to know what holds the man together . . . you apply a real jolt and see where the cracks appear."[19]

Today, such pleasures are called *lulz*. It's another form of social power. This popular catchphrase is used to express the enjoyment experienced when pranking someone or by posting offensive or disgusting content that will shock or offend others. As described in KnowYourMeme.com (www.knowyourmeme.com), an online website that documents Internet culture, "Scare prank reactions are yet another classic example of Internet users gunning for the lulz at the expense of close relatives and friends."

As a term, it is similar to the power dynamic that is at the heart of the German concept of *schadenfreude*. Psychologically, this German term (pronounced sha-den-froy-da) is often used in the English language without translation to describe the emotional response generated in feeling pleasure at another person's misfortune or suffering. A related concept is *ridicule,* a form of destructive humor that is a strategy for gaining social power.

Most forms of destructive humor are directed at particular individuals or groups of people who are perceived in a negative way. The target of ridicule fulfills an important task in the dynamics of the group. He or she is assigned all the weaknesses and illnesses of the group. By making the target the victim of disparaging humor, other group members can gain a feeling of superiority.[20] Intentional embarrassment is typically employed to establish or maintain power and control over others.

Many people have created scary maze game pranks. My colleague Silke Grafe and I decided to conduct a content analysis to see whether there were any cultural differences between German and American YouTube videos. We watched and coded 100 American and 100 German videos that we found by searching for the phrase "scary maze game." We found that while 27% of American YouTube videos feature a child under the age of 12 as the victim of the prank, only 7% of German videos feature children. With our own students, we reflected on these questions:

- What are the motives of an amateur video producer who uses young children's fear as a form of entertainment?
- Why are online videos featuring young children's fear responses more popular than those that feature a teen or older subject as the target of the prank?
- Could differences between American and German videos reflect cultural sensibilities of both the authors, the subjects, and audiences of YouTube videos?
- Do audiences bear any responsibility or obligation in their decision to view or not view these videos? Why or why not?

The Ethics of Representation

Art has the power to shape our sense of reality, which is why Picasso's aphorism, "Art is the lie that tells the truth," explains the function of art and culture in the realm of human experience. In the 19th century, when the novel was on the rise as a new art form, Samuel Taylor Coleridge introduced the concept of *the willing suspension of disbelief*, the idea that people can accept as real that which is illogical or improbable.[21] When we read a novel or view a fiction film, we are brought into the author's constructed world, which we actively interpret in relation to our own experience.

Online pranking videos provide a relatively safe and structured opportunity to explore *the ethics of representation.* When we use media, we can choose to treat the subjects represented as textual objects or we can choose to see them as representations of real people. If we treat them as objects only, then no ethical issues are raised. After all, YouTube videos are really just pieces of digital code, a string of 0s and 1s.

But if we acknowledge the human beings who are represented digitally, we must consider the point of view of the subject—the person, event, or experience that is featured.

Authors, audiences, and subjects are tied together in a complicated relationship of mutual dependence. After all, when you're filming someone (a subject), you are simultaneously participating in a real experience while you're creating a representation. Through the lens of the viewfinder, you create an illusion of the complex, three-dimensional, living, breathing, human being who is in front of the camera.

But as you create the film, you, the filmmaker, can control and shape how the subject is represented through editing. You have a form of social power that shapes how an audience experiences the subject. There we see that a clear ethical relationship emerges. Consider two examples from the many scary maze videos we viewed:

Example 1. A YouTube video depicts a teen boy pranking his mother. As she is playing the game but before she gets scared, she seems highly aware of the camera and even asks, "Are you going to put this on YouTube?"

Example 2. In this video, we see an older sibling pranking a 7-year-old, whose actions are being recorded via webcam. The child does not seem aware that the screen he is looking at is simultaneously recording his own reactions to the screen.

When exploring social power, the "Golden Rule" can be used to initiate meaningful conversation about social and ethical issues. In discussing these videos, we can ask the following:

- Should subjects have to give their consent before images that feature them are shared? Why or why not?
- How would you feel if someone created and shared an online video featuring a depiction of yourself that you felt was humiliating or embarrassing?
- What if you gave your OK but other people who viewed it thought it made you look stupid? Does that make a difference? Why or why not?

Young people are wrestling with these kinds of issues all the time because social networking sites like Facebook encourage people to represent both self and others in ways that bring social power to the forefront. Teens may have thoughtful and often sophisticated reasoning processes that reflect their decision making about what's OK and what's not. Dialogue about these issues builds critical thinking skills and gives teens a chance to reflect upon and articulate their values.

When we consider the point of view of the audience, the author, and the subject, the ethical triangle (Figure 7.2) enables us to address these questions:

Figure 7.2

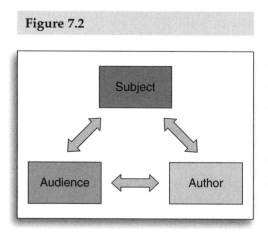

Subject

- *Consent.* Did the subject consent to the making of the media message?
- *Free Will.* Did the subject exercise free will in choosing to participate? Or was there coercion, where the subject was not truly free to refuse to participate?

Author

- *Intentionality.* Did the author act with goodwill toward the subject? Toward the audience?
- *Consequences.* Did the author consider the consequences of his or her actions on the subject? On the audience?
- *Social Good.* Does the effect of the author's actions contribute to furthering healthy social relationships and a just society?

Audience

- *Intentionality.* Did the user/viewer/reader/audience member have goodwill toward the author? Toward the subject?
- *Social Good.* Does the spectatorship experience contribute to furthering healthy social relationships and a just society?

When Self-Disclosure Reveals Problematic Behaviors

Classroom discussion like this may result in a student's *self-disclosure* about some aspects of his or her life online. Self-disclosure is the process by which one person lets his or her inner being, thoughts, and emotions be known to another. It is an essential part of personal growth and meaningful social relationships. Some of these disclosures may be predictable, others will be surprising, and a few may be problematic. Most parents and teachers have experienced this in one way or another. As a college teacher, I have had students reveal to me that discussions about media, sexuality, and gender helped them feel more confident in expressing their sexual orientation publicly. As a parent, my daughter and I had a conversation about why it's not appropriate to share with other friends a captured stream of highly personal instant messaging with another person that was conducted with the expectation that it was a one-on-one conversation.

Even in the best of circumstances, it's likely that teens will be attracted to the thrill of exercising social power and exploring the "dark side" of all that the Internet offers. Every young person will, at one time or another, fail to anticipate the consequences of his or her communication behavior. If students reveal these problems to you, consider it a sign of success. When teachers create learning environments characterized by trust and respect, that's when self-disclosure occurs.

When you talk about controversial online content with adolescents, you may learn about an online teasing or cyberbullying incident or the posting of an unflattering photo. You may learn about a parent's own addiction to the Internet or about a student who has been approached online by a potential predator. You may even discover that a student has had a cybersex experience.

During a conversation with middle-school students, one child described to me in great detail his experience downloading a Hollywood movie, a violation of copyright law. Another student bashfully revealed her screen name as "girlyblows14," explaining that she had discovered, through trial and error, that this screen name ensured that people would talk to her when she entered a chat room. These kids weren't boasting. They were sharing their experiences and asking for feedback. So I offered my thoughts and feelings, expressing my interpretation of their behavior without being judgmental or patronizing.

It can be both scary and exciting to transgress when you're a teen—it means you're acting independently and not controlled by your parents. It takes meaningful conversation with a trusted adult to discover that such thrills may come at a cost to one's sense of personal self-respect and social responsibility. Guidance and school counseling staff have significant opportunity to address these issues in the context of life at both school and at home.

It's possible that, in the context of talk about online social responsibility, a young person will disclose other forms of abusive or problematic behavior. Each year, more than three million cases of child abuse are reported and many more go unreported. Often such abuse may involve physical violence or sexual abuse by a family member. When teens disclose this behavior, it's important to listen carefully and not react with disgust or disbelief. Virtually every state requires doctors, teachers, day care providers, and law enforcement officers to report child abuse, so be aware that you may have a legal obligation to report what you learn.

Conclusion: Growing Up Online

Learning to live responsibly when it comes to online communication is a process. It's aided by support from caring adults. As a freshman in college, my son Roger wrote an essay titled, "Instant Message, Instant Girlfriend," which was published in the *New York Times* as part of the Modern Love series. There, he reflected on his experiences using the Internet in high school. He describes the power he felt when he discovered that he could manipulate his persona while online:

> Somewhere in the dark reaches of the Internet I went through a transformation sequence worthy of a Japanese children's cartoon. I suddenly shifted from an overweight, overdressed frog to a charming, handsome, technology-savvy prince. As soon as my fingers touched the keys, I was not just another face in an endless crowd. With words on a screen, I would never stutter. I could take as long as I wanted to think of the perfect answer to every question, and the perfect response to every flirtation. I was hooked. It was as if the Internet had

allowed me to turn flirtation and seduction into a video game. But I didn't know if my Internet charms were just a fluke or if they were real. I wanted, no, needed to know that the cool person I became when my fingers caressed the keys was actually me.[22]

Trying on this new identity through online communication helped Roger develop confidence in himself as a young man. But ultimately, his experience led to an "aha" moment when he discovered that playing at seduction created a lot of pain for the young women in his life who didn't know he was just experimenting with flirtation. He felt the need to break off his phony romances, realizing that he was "blinded by the common belief that somehow a relationship forged on the Internet isn't real. The Internet is not a separate place a person can go to from the real world. The Internet is the real world. Only faster."[23]

When we reinvigorate the humanities by using the pedagogies of digital and media literacy, our students gain the sense of wholeness called integrity. When our choices and actions, as both authors and audiences, match up to our values, we become humane, responsible, and effective communicators.

CHAPTER 7 LESSON PLAN

Online Relationships: Conducting an Interview

Overview: Select a friend, a family member, or another adult to interview about his or her experiences with online relationships. Take written notes to capture main ideas and details and then provide a summary of key ideas in paragraph form.

"Online relationships" include communicating via e-mail, text, video games, or social media sites like Facebook or Myspace. Interaction may be with the following types of people:

- People they know well (family and friends)
- People they work with (coworkers, colleagues, classmates)
- Acquaintances—People they have met briefly in the real world
- Online friends—People they have met online but not in person
- Online strangers—People they have interacted with online but do not know well

Name of Interviewee: _____

Relationship to Student: _____

Interviewee Signature: _____ Date: _____

QUESTIONS: Summarize what you learned from the interview in the space below.

1. What ways do you communicate with others using digital media (for example, cell phones, social networking sites, IM, chat, etc.)?

   _____

   _____

   _____

2. Have digital media ever affected your relationship with someone in a positive way? What happened?

   _____

   _____

   _____

3. What is the most annoying or difficult aspect about communicating with others using digital media?

_____

_____

_____

4. Have you ever had a misunderstanding with someone because of digital media? What happened? How did you resolve it?

_____

_____

_____

5. Write your own question here:

_____

_____

_____

Response:

_____

_____

_____

_____

_____

A full-sized reproducible of this worksheet can be found at www.corwin.com/ medialiteracy

TAKE ACTION

By Hamed Saber

8

What in the World

Teaching With Current Events

What You'll Find in This Chapter:

- Students explore controversial current events of local importance and demonstrate their understanding of choices and consequences by creating simple online video games about flash mobs in Philadelphia.
- By turning self-expression into a form of public participation, educators help students appreciate and understand global issues, natural and man-made disasters, and science news.
- Five essential concepts for understanding news help high school students understand journalism's role in the democratic practice of self-governance.
- There are special challenges when teaching with the unfolding narratives of current events, but when students get the opportunity to engage with news in ways that are meaningful to them, learning comes alive.
- Hands-on programs that help students create news for their school community give students a vibrant experience in thinking like a journalist.

Lesson Plan:

What's Newsworthy?

I n the spring of 2010, everyone was talking about the flash mobs in Philadelphia. Children, teens, and young adults, many of them African American, were using social networking tools on their cell phones to gather for informal fun that turned violent. The *New York Times* had reported that a "tsunami of kids" in aggressive and raucous form converged downtown "for a ritual that is part bullying, part running of the bulls." In the excitement of being in a large, spontaneous group of people, kids marched along with their friends, and some brawled with each other, others knocked over pedestrians, and a few vandalized property.[1]

Flash mobs, which had started in the early 2000s as a kind of playful social experiment meant to encourage spontaneity and illustrate the power of social media, had become an opportunity for children, teens, and young adults to explore the dynamics of risk-taking, peer pressure, and social power in an urban context.

When John Landis, a Russell Byers Charter School technology teacher, heard children talking at lunchtime about flash mobs, he recognized the opportunity to build a lesson plan around the news. Over the course of a few days, he selected news stories for his students to read, building their knowledge of events in Philadelphia and Washington, D.C. They learned that flash mobs were used for a variety of purposes, including political advocacy, informal play, and violence. They made a list of all the people who were interviewed for each news story. They read and deconstructed articles to discover how different points of view were included in the story: the teens involved, the police, and bystanders.

Using Red Lasso, an online TV news search engine, Mr. Landis and his students selected and watched several local TV news stories to view and discuss. Red Lasso (www.redlasso.com) enables users to search nearly live TV and radio content in over 150 cities across the United States. Users can search TV news and radio broadcasts by typing in keywords. They can make clips of stories, post clips to their blog or website, or send links to friends. The students looked at news stories and made a list of the common images: close-ups of flashing police lights and kids in handcuffs were common.

At the same time, Mr. Landis introduced students to key ideas about the structure of a news story and the reporting process. In the context of a natural process of questioning, students learned about how journalists identify sources. They learned about how quotes are chosen. They learned about what an assignment editor does and how video editing works. They learned about news values like timeliness, proximity, and conflict. Students visited the offices of the Philadelphia *Inquirer* to talk to editors about choices and consequences in the newsmaking process.

Choices and Consequences

As a technology teacher and video game player himself, Mr. Landis was familiar with how video games have been used to explore news and current events. There are many different types and styles of news games, but most are designed for older teens and young adults. Mr. Landis wanted to explore the relationship between journalism and the procedural literacy of computer programming, examining "the underlying situations that produce particular events, tracing their connection to larger social, political or economic situations."[2] After introducing students in the computer lab to some "serious games" like *Ayiti: The Cost of Life* (a simulation game about poverty in Haiti), he was intrigued about the possibility of helping students create their own games about topics of interest in news and current events. With his students, he introduced these questions: How do you take an issue like the flash mobs in Philadelphia and turn it into a video game? What parts of this story can be turned into a game? What were some of the choices involved? What were the consequences of each choice?

Using the free programming software Scratch (www.scratch.mit .edu), students developed many approaches to solve the design challenge at the heart of this assignment. Students worked individually or with a partner to create simple video games. As they planned their projects, they had deep discussions about choices and consequences, about violence, risk-taking, and danger, and about the stereotypes associated with being an African American teenager. Students shared their ideas and predictions about how police officers will behave and react under different circumstances.

Looking at the student projects, we can see the level of thoughtfulness and creativity that was activated by this assignment. Figure 8.1 shows an image from one student project. In it, a teen decides whether to go to a flash mob. The user gets to decide whether the character goes or stays home. If he stays home, he gets ridiculed and beaten up by his peers. If he goes to the flash mob, he must decide whether to vandalize property. If he breaks a car window, he gets arrested. If he doesn't break a car window, he also gets arrested. This student was aware that this particular point of view was completely absent from all the media accounts of flash mobs. In this video game, we see how the student expresses a no-win situation when it comes to the decisions about participating in flash mobs. Sadly, this reflects a too-common attitude about the often invisible but inevitable risks that African American children and young people in Philadelphia experience in the process of growing up.

Figure 8.1   A Flash Mob Video Game

In reflecting on his approach to support the creative work of students, Mr. Landis displayed sensitivity to the process of thinking about digital computing and creative skills in relation to larger issues about adolescent life skills and decision making:

> I didn't reject any ideas but played up the ones that got closer to the more implicit ideas at the heart of the news story. I hoped students would reflect the story's central paradoxes, and not just retell trivial elements of the narrative as a game. I wanted students to use the power of the interactive game to show how things might have occurred or could have been different if people made different choices. Plus, I wanted students to reflect on their own work as game designers. My most common question to them was: What choices are you giving the user?[3]

Mr. Landis wrote a press release about students' work analyzing flash mobs, and everyone was thrilled when a local TV news team showed an interest in the story. A cameraperson came to the school, interviewed the teacher and students and took pictures of the students talking, planning, and creating their projects. But when the 25-second story ran on NBC10, the Philadelphia local news channel, students had questions: Why had they not used their faces or voices in the news story? Why was the point of view of the teacher omitted?

One student counted how many times the phrase "flash mob" was used in the story. Another wondered the following: Was their learning experience just another excuse for the local station to recycle bad news? Why weren't their creative projects shown on a screen? One student noticed a tiny error in the broadcast: The reporter said the program was held "at" the university, but the program was actually held at the charter school, with the university as a sponsoring partner. Poor choice of preposition created an inaccuracy; in a teachable moment, the teacher discovered that through exploring this error, students could realize the importance of language in shaping our understanding of reality.

Educational experiences like this can link personal experience, historical knowledge, and rhetorical skills, deepening students' understanding of how social power and influence shape social action in ways that may propel social change. Howard Rheingold put it this way: "Listening to what young people care about is the necessary first step in enlisting their enthusiasm."[4] That's why teachers who want to promote civic engagement ask themselves this: What are young people curious about? What are they talking about? What are they asking questions about?

Incidental Learning From Entertainment

Activity: For one week, notice what you learn about the world from entertainment TV. To introduce this activity, you might use an excerpt from a show like *NCIS: Los Angeles* to demonstrate how concepts like the "black market" and "arms dealers" are explained. Encourage students to notice how *incidental information* about history, science, news, the law, technology, politics, and culture is built into many forms of entertainment. Invite students to keep a list near the TV and make notes about concepts and ideas as they watch. Each day, encourage students to recall specific examples and keep a list of the ideas that emerge.

News Is Everywhere: Learning From TV Entertainment

People of all ages learn about the world from television entertainment as well as from news. Each week, the characters and plots of entertainment TV shows and Hollywood movies convey information

In many middle schools and high schools, the polarized political climate has led to a withering away of civic education. Gone are the days when students clipped a newspaper article to bring in for current events day. Many teachers are afraid to give students such opportunities, fearful that they will bring in news stories about Britney's latest boob job or the drunken escapades of that overpaid professional athlete.

In some communities, it may be risky to develop activities where students actually take civic action. High school government courses stick to building knowledge of basic government functions. As Lance Bennett writes, "Most courses in public schools are thoroughly cleansed of the kinds of political issues and active learning experiences that young people might find authentic and moving."[9] But despite the challenges, there are many bright spots to be found in the work of talented teachers in schools all across the United States who are discovering ways to use digital media and technology to support civic engagement, "helping students to turn their self-expression into a form of public participation."[10]

Making Connections to World Culture

Getting in the habit of reading, listening, or viewing the news—in all its various forms—enables young people to flourish in the face of the vast information choices that surround them. In Seattle, Jessica Partnow, a Seattle educator, wanted her students to more deeply understand how news values are culturally inflected. In the context of a world culture class, she began one lesson by asking students to compare and contrast the English-language news monthly *Egypt Today* with *Newsweek*.

Both magazines had featured articles on the Israeli-Lebanese conflict. *Egypt Today* ran a several-page spread of full color photos depicting desperate people searching for friends and family in the dusty rubble of a freshly bombed apartment complex; another photo showed a dead body before it had been covered with a sheet. In contrast, *Newsweek* used an infographic as its main illustration: Stick figures in red and blue indicate the numbers of injuries and deaths on either side of the conflict.

In comparing and contrasting the two stories, students "respond to the idea that our media are sanitizing our information for us. They enjoy a rebellious, typical teenage reaction to being told what to think. Others pick up on the emotional manipulation inherent in printing pictures of extreme suffering—or in choosing not to print them."[11]

These discussions help students think about how—and who—is processing their information for them. And perhaps even more importantly, the lessons "foster a love for what she calls the 'mind-boggler,' or questions that do not have one simple answer—where wrestling with every side of the issue is what is most important."[12]

Ms. Partnow's students also interact with journalists and fellow students in the United States in an online project of the Pulitzer Center for Crisis Reporting (www.pulitzercenter.org). This emotionally powerful website provides students with information on global issues, helps them think critically about the creation and dissemination of news, and inspires them to become active consumers and producers of information. The program engages the next generation on pressing social, political, and economic issues around the world. Topics include women and children in crisis around the world, climate change, HIV/AIDS in the Caribbean, global water issues, and food insecurity. There are videos, lesson plans, and a social networking opportunity for students to respond and share ideas with journalists in countries all around the world, including Nepal, Jamaica, India, and Kenya.[13]

Understanding Journalism as Citizenship Training

These five concepts can support the development of critical thinking skills and enable students to understand journalism's role in the process of self-governance:

News Has Many Purposes

- To inform: News tells us about events, people, and problems in our neighborhoods, our country, and in the world.
- To persuade: News offers opinions that help us make up our own minds about complex and controversial topics.
- To entertain: News offers entertainment about novel and unusual things in the world that happened recently.

News Is Constructed

- Journalists make the news by getting ideas, information, and opinions from other people.
- They use a combination of moving images, language, sound, and pictures to express information in ways that are easy to understand.

- Through public relations, corporations, politicians, and ordinary people help make the news by actively reaching out to journalists and inviting them to cover what's important to them.
- To decide what's newsworthy, journalists use criteria like timeliness, proximity, relevance, conflict, and human interest.
- News editors must make choices because there is a lot of news and not much time. Deadline pressure affects what gets in the news.
- Journalists aim for fairness, accuracy, and balance. But there is inaccurate information in news reporting. Even a small word choice can make a message inaccurate. A lot of information is left out of a news report.

News Is a Business

- Journalists must balance what people need to know with what people want to know, because, to make money, attracting a large audience is vital.
- For TV news and newspapers, money from advertising provides most of the income to pay for salaries, technology, and supplies.
- Conflict and controversy increase the size of news audiences: Bad news is good for business.
- Today, some people get news directly from authoritative information sources by using the Internet. But because this can be time-consuming and difficult, many people rely on news organizations, aggregators, or bloggers.
- Online news aggregators are websites that retransmit news created by other news organizations. So much news is available for free today that news organizations are in crisis because it costs money to create quality news and journalism.

News Makes a Difference in the World

- News makes the unknown known. Publicity about a person, event, or product can create public visibility that translates into tangible and often highly valuable results. Bad news can destroy people's careers and their social relationships. Good news can increase votes, sales, or lead to new opportunities.
- News leads to political and social action. When information is revealed, people can respond. When we learn about an

environmental disaster, for example, people can do things to solve the problem. News creates opportunities for our society to improve and change.

- News can shape our opinions and feelings about people and places we don't experience directly, reinforcing or challenging stereotypes.

News Supports Civic Action

- News helps us make decisions about life: who to vote for, what to buy, what to do. The quality of information we have access to affects the quality of decisions we make.
- Anyone can be a journalist. No special license is required. Ordinary people can create a media message to reflect an experience of the world. People can use words, images, and interactivity to investigate and comment on what's happening in their community. This type of sharing becomes a form of civic action when others read or view it and respond.
- When people talk about the news, they share opinions, information, and ideas, which helps people learn, solve problems, and coordinate public action as citizens in a democracy.

Civic Engagement in Science

Social studies teachers are not the only ones who use news as a teaching tool. Science teachers also use the news in their classrooms, too. Studies show that more than 90% of high school science teachers use newspapers in some aspect of their science teaching. But most of the time, such use is incidental. When biology or chemistry teachers happen to come across an article, they may bring it into the classroom, but not in a systematic way as a formal part of instruction.[14]

News about science and technology affects nearly every aspect of our lives, from nutrition and exercise, decisions about cars, houses, and appliances, banking, travel, and more. Learning to be a critical reader of science news is perhaps one of the most important competencies students need to prepare them for a lifetime of learning. With the rapid explosion of the growth of new knowledge, people will need to be able to distinguish between high-quality and meaningful scientific research and junk science. That's why learning to read science news should be treated as a core learning activity, not an incidental activity that's done casually and at the margins of the classroom.

Making Time for Disaster News

Disaster news offers both an opportunity and a challenge for educators. War crimes and war coverage, hurricanes, earthquakes, mine explosions, floods, car crashes—all these events happen unexpectedly, disrupting the routines of daily life. They are never part of our curriculum plan—and yet, because of their intensity and emotional power, they can be a powerful learning opportunity if educators take advantage of them.

For example, during the BP oil spill of 2010, a teacher probed students' knowledge about the issues underlying the disaster before viewing and discussing a video from *PBS NewsHour* about the oil spill and its aftermath. What did students already know about offshore drilling? Why have some people argued for offshore drilling for oil? Why have some people argued against it? Why did President Obama announce his support for it in early April? What have been the major consequences of the catastrophe? Who has been impacted? How have the government and BP responded?

When teachers make time to discuss disasters in the classroom, it can build knowledge and skills, but it also can help support the development of empathy with others. Human development researchers point out the following:

> Parents, educators, and clinicians cannot leave it to the media to provide the clarifications that are necessary for young people to learn from a disaster. In times of disasters the media is focused on providing as much information as is possible to a largely adult audience. For something to come of this content that is of positive benefit for youth will require adults who moderate young people's media use by clarifying misconceptions, addressing reactions and concerns, and providing appropriate reassurance.[15]

Creating the News
as a Form of Civic Engagement

Many people believe that the Internet and digital technologies can turn people from passive spectators to active citizens, where people generate ideas that are relevant to their own communities. Technologically speaking, every person can be a pamphleteer. Peter Levine defines *public voice* as "any style or tone that has a chance of persuading other people (outside of one's intimate circle) about shared

Classroom Activities to Link
Current Events to Digital and Media Literacy

Digital and Media Literacy	Activity
Access: Find and select information.	Locate different types of current information online; find examples of news that is informative, persuasive, and entertaining.
Analyze: Identify author, audience, purpose, and point of view and examine the relationship between form and content.	Distinguish between straight news stories, features, and op-ed columns; compare and contrast points of view in different TV networks and in news stories over time.
Create: Compose or create a message using the processes of brainstorming, composition, and revision.	Interview a source to gather information, compose a photo montage, write a radio script, produce a video documentary, develop an opinion column.
Reflect: Connect to personal experience and stimulate curiosity.	Consider opportunities in your own life for making a difference and learn about young people whose actions or experiences are newsworthy.
Take Action: Share a message with an authentic audience for the purpose of making a difference in the world outside the classroom.	Develop a response to a current event and create a message to advocate for particular action, share ideas on a social network, develop a community action project.

matters, issues or problems."[16] That's what I mean when I use the concept of "taking action" in the process model for digital and media literacy education presented in Chapter 1.

There are two fundamentally different perspectives on the educational value of engaging students in the process of creating news and journalism. One perspective views it as a program that prepares students for future employment, helping young people gain vocational skills and internalize the occupational values and ideology of the profession. The other approach offers youth media as a way to educate supercitizens, armed with a critical eye, historical awareness, and substantial knowledge about the world around them.[17]

Each approach has its merits and its flaws. But ever since 1989, when the Supreme Court ruled that school administrators could legally censor student newspapers, I've become more aware of the real limitations of what students actually do learn from working at a school-sponsored newspaper. That's because the U.S. Supreme Court ruled in *Hazelwood v. Kuhlmeier* (1988) that principals could censor student media if they could demonstrate a legitimate educational reason to do so. The vague wording of the decision and the significant power imbalance between administrators and advisers have made it very difficult for teachers to serve as school newspaper advisors. For example, in March 2008, Linda Kane, the adviser of a high school newspaper in Naperville, Illinois, was told she would not be allowed to teach journalism or advise the paper the following year after students ran an article that administrators felt glorified drug use.[18]

In nearly 50% of American high schools, there are video production facilities where students take classes that help them learn how to use cameras, microphones, and editing equipment. Some of these programs are run as part of the vocational education program, alongside programs in cosmetology, automotive repair, and construction. In the most successful programs, students create videos for "businesses, weddings, little league games, athletic events, concerts, programs, festivals, parades, graduations, proms, and family reunions."[19] Some programs produce highlight tapes for athletic teams and individual highlight tapes for players to send to college scouts.

Fortunately, the best of these programs aren't just teaching students how to use the equipment but offering them the opportunity to use the power of media and technology to make a real difference in their communities. For example, Doug Green teaches broadcast journalism at Carlsbad High School near San Diego, California. He also founded the Student Television Network (www.studenttelevision .com), a national organization for high school broadcast journalism teachers.

In 2010, Mr. Green and his students were working on a documentary about hunger and food insecurity in their community, looking at food distribution centers for poor people and reflecting on how wealth and privilege may blind people to the real needs of poor families and children. Their production, titled *One in Seven*, traveled with a group of student leaders to Sacramento, California, and videotaped students testifying on behalf of military families who use the food pantries in San Diego. What a powerful learning experience for the students who participated in this project!

And of course, viewing the film could be inspiring to many young people around the country. But once their film is completed, Mr. Green's students will face another challenge: getting an audience to view their work in an increasingly crowded media environment. Putting up a video on YouTube does not guarantee that anyone will watch it. Even though more and more students are creating digital media using their blogs, wikis, cell phones, webcams, video cameras, and laptop computers, that doesn't mean that their peers, parents, or other adults in their communities (or around the world) are reading or viewing this work. That's why teachers whose students create digital media need to spend time exploring strategies for promotion and marketing to increase visibility for student media productions. And while teachers continue to rely on PBS and other educational media institutions for video materials for classroom use, they should look for opportunities in their own classrooms to screen and discuss a wide variety of high-quality student-produced multimedia.

Finding Youth-Produced Media Online

Adobe Youth Voices (www.youthvoices.adobe.com) is a global network of youth media makers in 32 countries. Users can view hundreds of high-quality short videos made by young people from around the world.

SchoolTube (www.schooltube.com) enables teachers to upload student-produced entertainment and informational videos at the website.

Listen Up! (www.listenup.org) connects young video producers and their allies to resources, support, and projects in order to develop the field and achieve an authentic youth voice in the mass media. Young people can upload their films to the Listen Up! website and see films made by other teens.

Media That Matters (www.mediathatmatters.net) is a showcase for short films on the most important topics of the day. For more than 10 years, this organization has helped young filmmakers reach larger audiences and inspired them to take action.

There's a natural egocentrism to adolescence. What that means is that some aspects of reflective thinking, empathy, and consideration of other people's points of view may be new and unfamiliar. Students can learn about the power of media to connect us emotionally to others and to express complex and multifaceted points of view when they create politically meaningful messages that reach real audiences. For example, one group of young filmmakers created a video titled, *No Child,* which highlights the role of military recruiters in American working-class high schools. Under the No Child Left Behind Act, schools are required to release information about students for recruitment purposes and may allow recruitment in the school building.

Youth director Gabe Cheifetz, and youth producers Glenn Scott and Chris "Shakademic" Johnson, interviewed both military recruiters and antimilitary activists, taking in a hidden camera to show how different persuasive techniques were used with potential recruits. When their film aired, the Army recruiter they had interviewed got in touch with the young filmmakers. In commenting on the film, Gabe Cheifetz writes about the recruiter's response to seeing the completed film:

> He was extremely offended by the piece, and felt that it was highly dishonest and that it was an attack on his profession. This was disturbing for me to hear, because I thought that he had argued his case persuasively, and generally came across well in the interview. He told me that people harass him, call him a baby-killer, and that recruiters are under immense pressure to hit recruitment goals. This is the big flaw in *No Child.* Talking to the recruiter, I realized that there is another side to the story, which is the pressure you're under as a recruiter to make the numbers. This is a key piece, and *No Child* should have showed it. It would have made it harder for audiences to watch *No Child* but would have been more of a complete story.[20]

Reflective thinking like this suggests that when young people recognize their power and their social responsibilities as communicators, they can experience significant personal growth.

Challenges in Teaching About News and Current Events

Students from across a wide spectrum of academic skills can engage with news and current events in ways that develop communication and critical thinking skills. Unfortunately, some teachers believe that only advanced students can engage with challenging contemporary issues and pedagogical approaches that put much of the classroom intellectual work on the students' shoulders.

But when high school students get sustained opportunities to make sense of and respond to news and current events in ways that are meaningful to them, learning comes alive. That's the premise behind a project developed by *PBS NewsHour*, produced by MacNeil/Lehrer Productions. PBS NewsHour Student Reporting Labs (www.student reportinglabs.com) connect high school teachers with local PBS affiliates to explore news and current events by producing short broadcast journalism packages. Working in a "cloud computing community," students upload drafts of their projects, get feedback from professional journalists, and then revise and share their videos with the world. Lesson plans help high school teachers explore key concepts and principles in journalism. At the end of this chapter, you'll find a simulation activity from *PBS NewsHour* where students recreate a TV newsroom's Morning Meeting to discover how editors make choices about what is newsworthy.

In one inner-city high school, researchers observed a classroom where students were making news and documentary videos about news and current events issues. These programs had a playful edginess, as students developed daytime talk shows (like *The Wendy Williams Show*) and reality-TV style documentaries (like the FOX program *Cops*). Students showed an appreciation of the formats and conventions of these types of programs as they enacted their own version. But the current events and political issues they discussed—urban crime, drug abuse, and law enforcement—were explored in a meaningful way, with students actively seeking information and offering a variety of opinions. In the context of extemporaneous dramatic collaboration, youth were participating in "a serious, heartfelt conversation between themselves with a depth of awareness of the legal system."[21]

David Cooper Moore has been examining how teachers respond when students introduce difficult topics from mass media, popular culture, or digital media—ones that transgress the boundaries of routine school topics. He observes that teachers intentionally or unintentionally choose when to *ignore, deflect,* or *engage* with the sometimes-provocative and difficult ideas that students bring into the classroom.[22] Thank goodness many classroom teachers have the courage and confidence to allow students space in the classroom for complex, controversial, and sensitive topics, using creative multimedia production strategies.

Of course, when educators do bring news and current events issues into the classroom, it may or may not make a difference. When done poorly, current events discussions can be just another reading comprehension activity. In many schools, news and journalism is often treated simply for its value in developing vocabulary skills.[23]

Low expectations create problems when teachers don't expect that young people will care about civic issues. When this occurs, some teachers may rely on lecturing, explanation, and recitation, which one scholar has conceptualized as *defensive teaching strategies*. This happens when teachers control knowledge and classroom interaction, summarizing texts on behalf of students in order to guarantee a particular interpretation.[24]

One researcher made a careful observation of six high school social studies teachers and found that although print and media texts are used in the classroom, teachers don't use news media texts in ways that build students' literacy and critical thinking skills. Observations revealed that many teachers summarized media texts both before and after students were asked to interact with the material. This eliminated the need for students to actually engage with and interpret the texts themselves. In this study, only 1% of activities in social studies classrooms included those that required students to analyze the content and format of media texts.[25]

When breaking news and current events are included as classroom texts, the lessons learned will never be ones that teachers can fully control. News often involves complex and unresolved social issues. When it comes to exploring news and current events in a global context, students may respond in different ways, depending on their background and life experience. They may be cynical, feel guilty, or become angry—and let's face it, that's not an unrealistic set of feelings. What with the state of health care, the justice system, the economy, the political system, the environment, and the inequalities that result from poverty, the challenges we face in our nation and the world today are vast.

When teaching with the unfolding narratives of current events, the content of the curriculum is inherently unstable and teachers cannot always anticipate the direction that the lesson will take. Therefore, educators need a community of practice that helps them develop confidence in taking the necessary and reasonable risks that engage young people in news and current events in ways that promote critical analysis, communication skills, and civic engagement.

CHAPTER 8 LESSON PLAN

What's Newsworthy?

Overview

Students first learn how decisions are made about what's newsworthy and then engage in a news simulation activity, conducting a Morning Meeting in the newsroom to decide the top stories for a TV newscast.

Learning Outcomes

By the end of this lesson, students will be able to do the following:

- Understand the difference between news and information
- Use news values to determine which stories are newsworthy
- Understand how a target audience shapes decisions about what's newsworthy
- Demonstrate collaboration, respectful listening, and participation in a group
- Use reasoning to select which types of news stories are most important for the public to know

Advance Preparation

Make copies of Worksheets A and B (see pages 164–166) for each team.

Engage Interest

Ask: How do editors decide what gets on the front page of the newspaper?

Listen to students' answers, which will reflect their prior knowledge of the practice of journalism. Ask students how they know what they know, since some students may be using a combination of ideas learned through direct experience or from family and friends, movies, TV shows, books, and other media.

Ask: What's the difference between "news" and "information"?

Answers will vary. You might want to make a Venn diagram to chart student answers, encouraging them to consider the similarities and differences between the two concepts. Emphasize that news is timely and current. News is relevant information that helps us understand what is happening in the world around us. News helps us in making decisions about our health and our finances and in playing our part in democracy at the local, state, and national levels.

Explore: What's News?

Pass out copies of Worksheet A. In this activity, students use a newspaper or go online to find examples of current news stories that use each of the five news values. Students will discover that important news stories may have multiple news values (i.e., they are timely, relevant, of local interest, feature human interest, and feature conflict or controversy).

Ask students to summarize a story they selected to represent each of the five news values. Use this activity to assess whether your students understand the five news values. Use "why" questions to promote reflective, critical thinking.

Consider the Target Audience

What's newsworthy depends on the target audience, to some extent. What's newsworthy to a 15-year-old will be different from that of a senior citizen. What's newsworthy to a city dweller may be less newsworthy to one who lives in a small town.

You may adapt this activity so that each team of students must select what's newsworthy for a specific target audience. For example, teams might pick the top three news stories for these different target audiences:

- Late-night TV viewers (generally young males and females, ages 15 to 30)
- People who live and work on the local army base
- Busy working mothers (generally ages 20 to 40)
- Sports fans

Observe that the concepts of "relevance" and "human interest" are most likely to change, depending on the characteristics of the target audience.

Key Ideas

Ask: What are the potential positive and negative consequences of news decisions that are based on the unique characteristics of the audience?

Listen carefully and write down students' ideas, putting them into two categories of positive and negative consequences. Allow time for students to dig in to this important and complex question. Encourage students to make a connection to their own experiences as news consumers on the many choices that are available to them through online media, television, radio, and print media.

Source: PBS NewsHour Student Reporting Labs (www.studentreportinglabs.com).

WORKSHEET A

PBS NewsHour Student Reporting Labs
What's Newsworthy?

News Values

When journalists talk about what's newsworthy, they rely on these five news values:

1. Timeliness	Immediate, current information and events are newsworthy because they have just recently occurred. It's news because it's "new."
2. Proximity	Local information and events are newsworthy because they affect the people in our community and region. We care more about things that happen "close to home."
3. Conflict and Controversy	When violence strikes or when people argue about actions, events, ideas, or policies, we care. Conflict and controversy attract our attention by highlighting problems or differences within the community.
4. Human Interest	People are interested in other people. Everyone has something to celebrate and something to complain about. We like unusual stories of people who accomplish amazing feats or handle a life crisis because we can identify with them.
5. Relevance	People are attracted to information that helps them make good decisions. If you like to cook, you find recipes relevant. If you're looking for a job, the business news is relevant. We depend on relevant information that helps us make decisions.

Instructions: Read and discuss these news values as a team. Then use a newspaper or go online to identify stories that fit into one or more of these five categories. Be prepared to explain why you made your choices.

A full-sized reproducible of this worksheet can be found at www.corwin.com/medialiteracy

WORKSHEET B

PBS NewsHour Student Reporting Labs
What's Newsworthy?

Morning Meeting Simulation

Instructions: In this role-playing activity, your team acts as editors and producers for a TV news show. After reading the choices that follow, discuss which stories should be the three top stories for your broadcast. The Executive Producer will expect team members to be prepared to offer a well-reasoned justification for their decision, using the five news values to explain their choices.

1. A fire claims the life of a family of five. Twelve firemen are injured while fighting the blaze and police are investigating it as a possible arson case.

2. President Barack Obama is hosting a birthday party/fundraiser for your local Senator, an incumbent Democrat who's locked in a tough campaign against a young Tea Party activist.

3. The Annual Turtle Race is being held at a local mall. It is an annual promotion for a national pet shop chain store that buys ads on your station.

4. Your local professional baseball team has just signed the nation's top high school recruit to the team.

5. A 24-car-accident occurred on the local highway. Ten people, including kids in a minivan coming back from a church field trip, were killed, and 25 were injured. Traffic was stopped on both ends of the interstate for five hours due to the accident.

6. Fifteen people were killed and 25 were injured when a suicide bomber went into a police station in Kandahar, Afghanistan. One of the dead soldiers was from your town.

7. Lady Gaga is playing a benefit concert for a homeless shelter. The sold-out show is expected to raise thousands of dollars to benefit the charity.

8. Two recent immigrants, one age 20 and another age 16, were killed in a shooting last night. Police believe the violence was gang related.

9. A local radio station is having a contest to see who can keep his or her hand on a new Mustang Convertible the longest. The winner gets to keep the car. About 100 people have been there since the contest started last night.

10. A popular pro basketball player is unveiling his new brand of sneakers at your local mall.

11. A new research study shows that people who eat at McDonalds three times a week die five years earlier than people who don't.

12. Your community has passed its annual budget, which includes dramatic cuts to the health and safety programs for senior citizens, who make up more than 30% of the residents in your community.

9

Infusing Digital and Media Literacy Across the Curriculum

What You'll Find in This Chapter:

- School leaders and passionate teachers, armed with good ideas, can be inspiring to other colleagues, but respect for diverse motivations is key.
- Whether offered as a stand-alone course or integrated within existing curriculum, digital and media literacy education can be most effective when it is designed to maximize the specific resources available in the school district and community.
- Collaboration among classroom teachers, technology specialists, and school library/media specialists provides elbow-to-elbow support that helps people master and internalize new skills.
- Internet filtering, censorship policies, and ignorance of copyright law can interfere with effective digital and media literacy education.
- Digital and media literacy education helps educators discover the capacities of students who normally do not fare well in traditional classroom settings.

U ndoubtedly by now you realize that digital media, mass media, and popular culture are powerful resources for educators that need to be integrated into education across all subject areas. In this chapter, I look at the process of school change to examine the kinds of programs, institutional support structures, and policies that help get digital and media literacy infused into the curriculum in Grades 7–12. In writing the book, I have selected a handful of vignettes to describe some of the many talented middle-school and high school educators I have met over the years. Teachers from kindergarten to graduate school are using digital and media literacy in the classroom success-fully. But they didn't do it alone. They worked collaboratively, strate-gically, to build programs that fit the needs of their students and their school communities. There's no one-size-fits-all recipe for success—but in this chapter, you'll get ideas that will help you build capacity for developing and implementing programs and policies that work.

Why It Matters

It all starts from a place of passion. Some people say that digital and media literacy gets under your skin, because once you discover how well it works with learners, you want every student in the world to experience it. It turns out that teacher advocates have always been a source of innovation in education. A passionate teacher, armed with a good idea, can be tremendously inspiring to other colleagues. Many current district-level digital and media literacy efforts started because a diverse group of passionate teacher advocates came together to work collaboratively toward accomplishing a goal.

When teachers use mass media, digital media, and popular culture to address social, political, and cultural issues, students develop the capacity to make sense of and critically analyze the world around them. When students use digital media to create, they synthesize ideas and information to experience a feeling of genuine mastery and ownership that promotes intellectual curiosity. When they share ideas using digital media, students gain a sense of social responsibility as they contribute to improving their communities and the world around them. Connecting to others and participating in a shared dialogue helps us continue to learn—whether that be in formal or informal situations, in face-to-face interactions, or through e-mail, Twitter, Facebook, or blogs.

One of the reasons why there is increasing momentum for digi-tal and media literacy as a *community education movement* is that educators have a variety of different motives for bringing it to their students. See Figure 9.1 for a list of the most common motivations

Figure 9.1 Motivations for Digital and Media Literacy

Your Motivations for Digital and Media Literacy

Educators have many different motivations for integrating media and technology into their work with students. What motivations are important to you? Review the list that follows and rank order the top five that most closely relate to your goals and motives:

_____ to modernize the curriculum and make it more relevant to students

_____ to strengthen students' ability to resist the negative messages present in mass media, digital media, and popular culture about violence, materialism, stereotypes, and sexuality

_____ to improve students' writing and communication skills by enabling them to use a wide range of message forms, symbol systems, and technologies

_____ to promote creativity and self-expression

_____ to increase student motivation and engagement in the classroom

_____ to build students' appreciation for the function of journalism, news, and information as tools for citizenship in contemporary society

_____ to build students' ability to be active, thoughtful "readers" or interpreters of the media messages in their cultural environment

_____ to help students use their own voices for advocacy and social change

_____ to strengthen discrimination skills in distinguishing between high-quality and low-quality messages

_____ to increase students' knowledge of the mass media in society

_____ to build appreciation for film and visual media as an art form

_____ to develop students' skills in using digital technology tools

_____ to promote appreciation for locally produced media and respect for diverse cultures

_____ to support the development of students' content knowledge

_____ write your own reason

---

among educators in Grades 7–12. Depending on your background, interests, and life experience, you may decide that some of these motives are more important than others. Which ones are most important to you?

In building coalitions, it is important to respect and honor our varying priorities and find partners who can both support and challenge us. While one teacher might be drawn in by an interest in social justice, another teacher may want to help students appreciate film and visual media as an art form, and someone else might want to cultivate a climate of respectful and civil behavior among adolescents in their online social interactions. One educator may be jazzed about helping kids tell their own stories, valuing the use of technology or social media tools for project-based and collaborative learning. Another may want to reach disengaged or special education learners, and still another may appreciate students' ability to be active, thoughtful readers, critics, or interpreters of the media messages in their cultural environment. Fortunately, the flexibility of digital and media literacy instructional practices supports this diversity in our motives and big-picture goals.

When students explore digital media, mass media, and popular culture, it opens up the arena of teaching ethics and values. Digital and media literacy education can explicitly address both the moments of transcendence that occur when we are moved deeply by a film, a book, a video game, an ad, or a song, as well as those mediated experiences that disturb and trouble us, like YouTube fight videos, Holocaust denial sites, or political ads that exploit people's fears. The themes and issues found in popular culture represent both the abundant trivialities and the deeply meaningful aspects of our life experiences as human beings. As we have seen in this book, everyone has an interest in both *protecting* and *empowering* students for life in a participative and highly mediated society with an ever-growing array of opportunities to share and learn.

Enlightened Leadership

Leadership and vision are critical components of the process of bringing digital and media literacy to secondary education. School leaders can inspire educators by helping teachers make large and small steps toward embracing new ideas and instructional practices. That's what principal Troy Czukoski did at Phoenixville (PA) Middle School. When he learned about digital and media literacy, he brought the concept to his faculty and helped them develop a new elective. When Jessica Brown, principal of the Arts Academy at Benjamin Rush High School in Philadelphia got the opportunity to write a mission statement for her school, she knew it was important to connect the fine and performing arts and literacy, so she prioritized a focus on visual and media literacy skills for the whole school. When Len Ference of Mechanicsville (PA) Middle School learned about a conference for integrating media literacy into middle-school health education and English language arts, he encouraged his teachers to attend. At the Science Leadership Academy in Philadelphia, high school principal Chris Lehmann supports teachers as they implement digital and media literacy into the subject areas, promoting students' intellectual, social, and emotional development. According to Lehmann, to implement new ideas, teachers need time to learn and play—through a weeklong summer gathering, weekly faculty workshops, and common preparation time for teachers during the school day.

As I've shown in this book, teachers also need support for the kind of *planful* and *strategic risk-taking* that enables student voices and students' experience with mass media, popular culture, and digital media to enter the classroom. To implement digital and media literacy wisely in K–12 education, careful decision making is needed, and this is best done through a collaborative process that involves school leaders, faculty, library/media and technology staff, parents, and other stakeholders. [1] Consider the following practical strategies that can be employed by school leaders to build digital and media literacy into the curriculum. Here are some of the most common options, choices, and decisions that educators must make as they discover how best to bring digital and media literacy into their schools.

Integrate Digital and Media Literacy Within Existing Curriculum

Should digital and media literacy be offered as a separate stand-alone course or should it be integrated into the curriculum's existing subjects? That's one of the seven great debates in the media literacy movement.[2] Whether a school or district uses an *integration model* or *stand-alone approach* (or a combination of both) should depend on the human, material, and other resources available. There are excellent examples of stand-alone programs in many American high schools and equally strong examples of programs that use an integrated approach.

When teachers infuse digital and media literacy across the curriculum, it requires that educators use texts—including textbooks, newspapers, TV shows, magazines, books, movies, videos, games, and online resources—beyond their function as conveyors of information. This approach carries with it the potential for all students in a school to gain exposure to digital media use, media analysis, creative collaboration, and hands-on production activities.

But this approach has limitations. When integrating digital and media literacy into the subject areas, it's possible that superficial uses of digital media and technology may trivialize the practice of accessing, analyzing, composing, reflecting, and taking action. In addition, when all teachers are responsible for teaching something, then no one is really responsible. As one scholar put it, with media literacy concepts permeating the curriculum, it may "always be at the margin of each subject, as a more or less unrelated, unvalued extra."[3] When a topic, issue, or skill is supposed to be developed across the curriculum, it may end up invisible.

Still, plenty of educators are finding ways to integrate digital and media literacy into the secondary curriculum. For example, Val Knobloch, a technology integration specialist, helps support educators in his service area, which includes 29 school districts in west central Wisconsin. He provides support to educators who are interested in integrating digital and media literacy practices into their existing curriculum. With his support, many teachers have worked with their students to produce a newspaper, TV news program, or video yearbook.

When they received an Enhancing Education Through Technology (EETT) grant in 2006, Val recognized that simply providing teachers with technology training does not necessarily translate into technology integration. The grant made it possible for a teacher and a library media specialist to be available in each of 28 rural school districts in northwestern Wisconsin for one school year. Working collaboratively, the teachers integrated multimedia technology into their classrooms through the production and implementation of project-based learning. Teachers need a community of support to aid them in exploring the full range of possibilities associated with using digital and media literacy in the classroom.

Create Separate Courses and Programs in Digital and Media Literacy

Some schools have adopted a strategy of developing a separate course for digital and media literacy or used afterschool programming or summer classes as a place to focus on this work. For example, at Summit High School in New Jersey, school leaders and teachers renovated part of their high school to create a Media Literacy Center with professional grade cameras and a computer lab. English supervisor Corey Walsh notes that the elective, "21st Century Media," gives students opportunity to explore both critical analysis and creative production in a more formal and focused way. These types of electives generally emerge in schools when there is deep interest from a teacher with specialist knowledge or competencies. Courses like this can be rich and substantive. But one of the downsides of this approach is that stand-alone courses in digital and media literacy are generally available to only a tiny proportion of students, not the whole population.

However, some stand-alone programs do reach all students in a district. For example, when teachers at Concord High School in Concord, New Hampshire, decided to infuse media literacy into the curriculum, they sat down together as a faculty and asked themselves the following: What do we want students to know and be able to do when it comes to media and communication skills? After a process that included shared reading and discussion, they created a required Grade 11 English course, Media/Communications, that brought their vision forward.[4] For nearly 15 years, this course has enabled every student in the school district to develop the kind of critical thinking, collaboration, and communication skills that are described in this book.

Some programs reach only the best and brightest students in a school district. For example, at Montgomery Blair High School in Silver Spring, Maryland, the program emerged from a deep interest in developing a cross-disciplinary program that connected English, history, and the media arts. The Communication Arts Program (CAP) began in 1987 and is now one of the premier examples of a secondary school integrating media analysis and media production into the subject areas of language arts and social studies. It is an application-based program that attracts talented students from across the district.

During their junior and senior years, CAP students select their best work in a variety of categories (including writing skills, media literacy skills, and social awareness) that was completed for classes that are a part of the program's curriculum. After students have put together their portfolio to the satisfaction of CAP faculty members, they undergo a public interview process where they present and discuss their work in front of a board of community residents and other experts.

In the CAP program, students participate in interdisciplinary projects that connect English language arts, social studies, and media classes in Grades 9, 10, and 11. For example, 10th-grade students peer into their "crystal ball" to research demographic and voter characteristics and then predict the presidential, U.S. Senate, U.S. House of Representatives, and gubernatorial races throughout the United States. The students' predictions are presented to the *Washington Post* for inclusion in the newspaper's political prognostication contest in which students compete against professional political pundits. One year, students even beat the experts!

Based in part on the success of the CAP program, in the 2004–2005 academic year, Montgomery Blair High School inaugurated a series of small learning communities to meet the needs of students not enrolled in special magnet programs. One was the Media Literacy Academy. Now any student in the high school can select to enter this small learning community. In Grade 10, students take an "Introduction to Media Literacy" course, which introduces critical thinking skills and links to health issues such as media violence, sexuality, body image, and issues of representation. Students take electives in media production (including broadcast journalism, print journalism, or web design) in Grades 11 and 12. During their senior year, students also take a required capstone "Media and Society" course and complete an internship or independent research project.

Mentoring From Technology Specialists and Library/Media Professionals

It's not easy to learn new technology skills and instructional practices when you have five periods a day to teach. Much of the best work in digital and media literacy occurs as a result of productive collaboration between classroom teachers, technology specialists, and library/media professionals. Joyce Valenza, librarian at Springfield Township High School in Pennsylvania, says it's never been a better time to be a library/media specialist. She uses remix videos to help students understand concepts of intellectual property, copyright, and fair use and helps students develop nuanced search strategies using Google Alerts, library databases, and new forms of information, including inspiring speeches from thought leaders who present at TED talks.[5]

School library/media professionals and technology coaches, working together, can often provide the kind of *elbow-to-elbow support* that helps teachers master and internalize new skills. For example, over a three-year period, the Classrooms for the Future (CFF) initiative supported such partnerships in over 500 Pennsylvania high schools. Evaluation data showed that with the appropriate kinds of support, teachers were able to transform some teaching practices. Observation results indicate that students spent more time working independently, working in groups, and talking with the teacher one-to-one or in small-group conversations. In the third year, researchers found that significantly less time was spent in teacher lecture or demonstration and in teacher-led low-level discussion, while significantly more time was spent in project-based learning.[6]

School library/media professionals can have a powerful impact on teaching and student performance. For example, at Avon Middle High School in Massachusetts, seventh graders take a class titled "Information Literacy," where digital and media literacy concepts are put into practice. In other schools, school library/media professionals support teachers as they begin to integrate digital media and technology tools into the curriculum. But adequate administrative and financial support for school library programs is not always available in American schools. Unfortunately today, a growing number of schools lack certified library media specialists. A survey of Wisconsin K–12 library media programs showed that programs that had full-time professional and support staff exhibited a greater impact on student academic performance. Top performing schools had nearly 1.5 times more library media program staff per 100 students and about twice as many staff hours per 100 students than low-performing schools.[7]

University faculty and students, local nonprofit organizations, local cable access centers, and media arts and cultural institutions can also be meaningful partners for school districts and teachers. At the Media Education Lab at Temple University, we've been exploring how undergraduate and graduate students can support students and teachers in K–12 schools. College students majoring in communication work with classroom teachers who are integrating digital and media literacy into existing subjects. It's a win–win for both of them as college students get a taste of community service in working with teachers and students and schools get the talent and energy of young people who are skilled users of digital media.

Respect for Student Voice

A deep commitment to student voice is at the heart of digital and media literacy.

When students have opportunities to actively participate in dialogue in the classroom, their writing improves. That's because classroom discussion is a vital part of the brainstorming and prewriting process. The concept of student voice is also implicated in how students are able to influence the progress of their own lessons. As one scholar put it, "By inviting students to become more equal partners in classroom discourse, expectations for students as thinkers and learners are elevated, and students are encouraged to become engaged in their studies. In addition, when students are allowed to choose their own readings, they are likely to become more deeply engaged in their academic work."[8]

Truth be told, it's not as easy as it sounds. Teachers need to be confident and skillful in managing dialogue, inspiring and motivating participation, bringing out the quiet voices, toning down the loud and abrasive ones, addressing conflict, and promoting critical thinking in ways that support and promote learning. You've seen many of these strategies illustrated in the previous chapters of this book.

But teachers don't always respect students' interests and concerns. We don't always ask good, open-ended questions that engage learners or even stop talking long enough to give students time to share their own ideas. And when it comes to the use of digital technology in the classroom, research reveals that even young preservice teachers (who have been using technology their whole lives) experience feelings of bewilderment. They may also experience fear of using technology and may take comfort in traditional forms of structured student–teacher interaction. These feelings and behaviors may interfere with the types of student-centered learning activities that support the development of student voice.[9]

Without coordinated and sustained support from teachers and school leaders, it can be difficult for digital and media literacy initiatives to thrive in high schools. For example, in one urban high school in Philadelphia, a young teacher was working with her students to create short documentary videos about social issues that were meaningful to them. A group of students had picked as their topic the problem of school security-student relationships at the school. Like many schools in urban communities, this school was 1 of 25 persistently dangerous schools in the city and it had a large school security staff. (In the School District of Philadelphia in 2009–2010, there were 1,394 dangerous incidents, including aggravated assault, rape, robbery, and possession of a weapon.) Relationships between school security staff and students were deteriorating as students felt disrespected by the staff. Students conducted video interviews with fellow students, teachers, and school security officers to understand and document their experiences. From the interviewing process, they learned the school security officers truly wanted to be helpful to students, since their job was to keep them safe. But the cycle of disrespect was creating problems for them, too.

Students contacted the school principal to schedule an interview to discuss the issue. They wanted to conduct an on-camera interview they could use in their documentary. The principal agreed to meet with students for their video production. But first one meeting was cancelled, and then another, and still another. As their deadline approached, students became more and more depressed. Could they even make a plausible documentary without representing the point of view of the principal? Was this the principal's way of dismissing their project? Would she ever support a public screening of their project once it was completed? In the end, the students' video production fizzled in midproduction. The principal's multiple cancellations of the interview sent a clear message, whether intentionally or not. Students had become demoralized, no longer believing that their attempt to create a video to address the communication problem between students and school security could ever accomplish its intended goal.

By contrast, other school leaders go to great lengths to champion student expression. At Montgomery Blair High School, students have a significant amount of editorial independence that has long been protected and respected by the community. Student voice is valued. The school has an array of student media production resources, including a school newspaper, student-produced website, and television production program. *Silver Chips* is the school's independent student newspaper, with both print and online components. Blair Network Communications (BNC) is a student-run multimedia organization and an academic class. BNC is divided into five divisions with a student serving as the executive director for television, radio, production engineering, Internet, and public relations (www.bnc.mbhs.edu). Working collaboratively, students produce two 30-minute shows that are broadcast countywide through local cable access. One show, titled *Metropolitan*, is a 30-minute show that discusses happenings in the Washington, D.C., area. The show features interviews with local figures, video segments, and in-studio discussions. They also produce a daily, six-minute morning announcement program for the school.

Back in 1996, Blair students produced a live television documentary featuring a debate on same-sex marriage. They had no idea that the superintendent got flak from some people in the community and had used the incident to alter the guidelines for school-sponsored student media. Without the knowledge or approval of the school board, he inserted language into the guidelines that gave school officials greater authority to control school-sponsored student expression. That language stated that material could be banned if it "associates the school with any position other than neutrality on matters of political controversy."

Taking their case to the school board and the *Washington Post,* courageous teachers spoke out on behalf of student voice. They said that in order to learn to be responsible citizens, students need the same freedom of expression that U.S. citizens have. The board of education removed the language from the guidelines, which had stated that material could be censored if it advocated activities that are not "shared values of our society."[10] In Montgomery County, this experience was a major victory for student voice. In schools across the country, teachers and students must continue to work together to protect their civil rights to free expression—in the classroom and online.

Technology Policies

Many educators have a love–hate relationship with the Internet filtering at their school. Some technology leaders at school have separate portal filters that enable teachers to access social media like Facebook, Flickr, and YouTube, while prohibiting those services to students. Some have rigid rules and may not respond to teachers who request that specific sites be unblocked. I have personally visited more than a couple of schools where I can't display the curriculum available online at my own website at the Media Education Lab (www.mediaeducationlab.com) because the filtering software has blocked it!

Some (but not all) states have formal policies about how the Internet in school is regulated. In Virginia, public schools are required to adopt Internet use policies that (1) prohibit transmitting or viewing illegal material on the Internet, (2) prevent access by students to materials the school deems harmful, and (3) select technology to filter or block child pornography and obscenity. In Georgia, public schools must adopt and enforce reasonable policies of Internet safety that will protect children from access to harmful material, and schools cannot receive state funds unless it implements and enforces an acceptable-use policy.

The issue of Internet filtering in schools is a great topic for high school students to explore. I was working on a curriculum project for a high school that involved students' learning about some controversies regarding the Internet in education. As part of the curriculum, I intended to have students learn about the legal and political issues associated with Internet filtering in public schools and libraries. Internet filtering in schools is controversial among library media specialists, technology specialists, and school board members. In my curriculum plan, after learning about the historical and political context, students would stage a debate about whether there should be Internet filtering in their school. As I developed the plan, I was concerned about designing the debate so that high school students could be able to argue a variety of positions. Wouldn't every kid naturally want unfiltered Internet access in school?

When I shared my concerns with my then 17-year old daughter, Rachel, she said, "Mom, I'm so glad our school doesn't allow us to use Facebook in school. I am totally in favor of Internet filtering in school. Without it, I would never be able to get any homework done." I was so surprised, you could have knocked me over with a feather!

In collaboration with students, parents, faculty, and school leaders, each school and community needs to develop an effective policy for acceptable use of technology that works for the needs of their students. Too many schools and educators are fighting a losing battle with cell phones, iPods, social media, and other technology devices. After all, when you have a computer in your pocket, you're going to want to use it. As we have seen in this book, educators can help students learn how to use media texts and technology tools appropriately and responsibly.

When it comes to cell phones, educators in some schools are discovering that policies based on respect and courtesy have a bigger positive impact than those based on control and prohibition. Doug Fisher and Nancy Frey write about a shift their high school made in replacing the technology policy with a courtesy policy. Figure 9.2 shows the policy. Simply put, students are expected to use their technology *when it's appropriate*. When the new policy was implemented, students were thrilled that they could send text messages and listen to music between classes, during lunch, and during class when doing independent work. The policy changed the school climate because students got feedback about their actions rather than punishment for breaking the rules.[11]

Censorship Policies

In many high schools, teachers make the judgment call on whether to show PG-13 or R-rated films or to read books with sexuality, violence, or other controversial content in the classroom. Some teachers issue permission slips to students prior to reading a book or viewing a film that may be controversial, some teachers permit students to choose the books they read, and other teachers use the fast-forward button on the remote control to skip over objectionable parts of films.

Figure 9.2 Courtesy Policy

Health Sciences High and Middle College

Courtesy is a code that governs the expectations of social behavior. Each community or culture defines courtesy and the expectations for members of that community or culture. As a learning community, it is our responsibility to define courtesy and to live up to that definition. As a school community, we must hold ourselves and one another accountable for interactions that foster respect and trust. Discourteous behaviors destroy the community and can result in hurt feelings, anger, and additional poor choices.

In general, courtesy means that we interact with one another in positive, respectful ways. Consider the following examples of courteous and discourteous behavior:

Courteous	Discourteous
• Saying please and thank you • Paying attention in class • Socializing with friends during passing periods and lunch • Asking questions and interacting with peers and teachers • Asking for, accepting, offering, or declining help graciously • Allowing teachers and peers to complete statements without interruption • Throwing away trash after lunch • Recycling materials and placing all trash in appropriate bins • Cleaning your own workspace • Reporting safety concerns or other issues that require attention to a staff member	• Using vulgar, foul, abusive, or offensive language • Listening to an iPod during a formal learning situation such as during a lecture or while completing group work • Text messaging or talking on a cell phone during class time • Bullying, teasing, or harassing others • Corporal punishment • Hogging bandwidth and/or computer time • Not showing up for your scheduled appointments or completing tasks • Failing to communicate when you're not coming to school

Consequences for engaging in discourteous behavior may include restoring the environment, meetings with staff or administrators, the development and implementation of a behavioral contract, removal of privileges, and/or suspension/expulsion from the school.

Source: Health Sciences High and Middle College Student Handbook, p. 10.

In some communities, the superintendent and the administration have lost confidence in teachers' judgment to make these decisions. That's because of some spectacularly bad decisions on the part of some teachers, who may use movies as a reward for good behavior, take the kids to the computer lab as a break from "real" learning, or use music, media, or technology to keep disruptive classrooms quiet and orderly. Nearly all educators are aware of these nonoptimal uses of media and technology—and these are practices that do not promote digital and media literacy learning.[12]

That's why some schools require prior approval of DVDs before viewing in the classroom. In some schools, movies must be submitted in advance to undergo a review process. In other schools, there is blanket rule: No R-rated films can be screened. There are, however, real educational consequences of these rules.[13] For example, a teacher whose students read John Steinbeck's *Of Mice and Men* won't be able to view the 1992 film adaptation starring John Malkovich and Gary Sinise, since that movie is rated R. The problem is that several R-rated films like *Schindler's List* or *One Flew Over the Cuckoo's Nest* are valuable texts in history and English classrooms in senior high schools across the country. Over time, the ratings system has changed as depictions of sexuality and violence have become more normative. Films that were rated R in the 1980s would be unlikely to receive that rating today.

As we've seen in this book, teachers show video excerpts and even whole films throughout middle and high school in order to support the teaching and learning process. Teachers know that films open up discussion in ways that engage students. These types of censorship policies limit teachers' ability to bring digital and media literacy into the curriculum. Educators need to work together to correct misuses of media and technology so that movies, games, and videos are used for truly educational purposes.

Advocating for Copyright and Fair Use

Helping young people become socially responsible users of digital media is perhaps one of the most important motives for integrating digital and media literacy into the curriculum in Grades 7–12. In a previous book, *Copyright Clarity: How Fair Use Supports Digital Learning*, I explain why educators with interests in digital and media literacy need to educate themselves and their students about their rights and responsibilities under copyright law. Our culture is in a time where the concept of authorship and ownership are in transformation, and K–12 educational leaders need to participate as advocates in ensuring that the law continues to support the essential and timeless values of education.

That's why I was delighted when a new ruling from the U.S. Copyright Office affects how students and teachers can use digital material in the classroom. The change is part of a new interpretation of the Digital Millennium Copyright Act (DMCA), a U.S. copyright law that criminalizes production and dissemination of software, devices, or services intended to circumvent the digital rights management technology that controls access to copyrighted works.

I was one of a handful of educators who presented a formal petition to the Copyright Office in 2009 to receive an exemption that would allow educators and students to legally "rip" excerpts of copy-protected movie DVDs for comment and criticism in media or film studies classes. *Ripping* is the process of copying audio or video content to a hard disk, typically from removable media. According to the Copyright Office, college-level instructors and students in media studies/communication classes can now legally unlock a DVD to make excerpts from copyrighted materials or create "remix" videos for purposes of commentary and criticism.

Before the new ruling, the DMCA made it illegal to rip portions of DVDs by bypassing the copy-protection code on a disc using easily available software programs unless the user qualified for a special exemption given in 2006 to film professors—the only educators who were legally entitled to rip film excerpts from movies owned by their department libraries for teaching and learning.

The Copyright Office wanted to limit the exemption only to those groups who could prove a reasonable harm and who could demonstrate that bypassing encryption is the only way to accomplish fair-use purposes. In the ruling, the Copyright Office indicated that K–12 educators, who generally don't need the highest quality clips for classroom use, can make screen captures of copy-protected content.

Thank goodness that the Copyright Office clarified the legal use of screen capture tools for fair use. Screen capture tools such as Jing (www.techsmith.com/jing) let users make a copy of any action on a computer screen. If you play a copy-protected DVD on your computer, you can make a copy of an excerpt using screen capture. You can select the whole screen or part of the screen to make a copy of a YouTube video, for example. These clips can then be saved as digital files on a computer.

But when student work is submitted to film festivals or designed to be viewed on the big screen, then high-quality images are essential. In these cases, the Copyright Office allows nonprofit users (even K–12 students and teachers, presumably) to unlock DVDs when using short excerpts to create videos for purposes of comment and criticism. Educators should feel confident that their use of copyrighted materials for teaching and learning is supported by the doctrine of fair use.

Compose a Critical Commentary of a Video Using Screen Capture Software

Activity: Students develop a critical analysis video, combining their own commentary with a short segment of an existing online video to create a simple media production using screen capture software.

1. **Preproduction.** Work with a partner to find an appropriate online video to analyze. View it carefully, using the five critical questions to make notes of key ideas. Then compose a short script that is under three minutes in length. Be sure it has an engaging opening and a powerful conclusion.

2. **Production.** Rehearse and practice while viewing a segment of video in order to match up the images and the language in your script. Look for places where you can pause to insert some sound from the online video. If your computer doesn't have a webcam, you'll need to use a microphone with your computer. Then perform your script orally, using the software to capture the moving image on your computer screen and your voice.

3. **Postproduction.** Use video editing software to create a title and add credits. Share with the world!

Reaching All Learners

Teachers have different priorities when they work with people of different ages. Elementary school teachers are deeply committed to teaching children. As we move across the life span, the focus shifts away from learners and onto subject areas, content, and disciplinary knowledge. College professors are, first and foremost, teaching subjects. That's partly why so many students fail to graduate from college—there are various hoops to jump through, gates and barriers that weed out many who "don't have what it takes" to do college-level work.

One of the reasons why I value digital and media literacy education is that it continues to help me discover the capacities of students who normally do not fare well in traditional classroom settings. For example, one of my students, whom I shall call Joyce, smiled a lot and nodded in my class, but she didn't show much promise in responding to open-ended questions or developing her ideas in writing. It wasn't until Joyce participated in a simple media composition activity that I could really discover who she was as a person. Early in the semester, I sometimes use media composition projects as a *diagnostic tool,* a way for me to learn more about the strengths and talents of my students and to see the areas of growth needed.

When my undergraduate students created a simple media project using screen capture software to critically analyze a children's TV show using the five critical questions of media literacy, Joyce worked with a partner to write a short script, record the voiceover, and align it with some video from a PBS program, *WordGirl,* a children's program that teaches vocabulary.

After some resistance and hesitation, Joyce agreed to perform the voiceover, with little practice or preparation. To the surprise of all of us, Joyce's performance was captivating. Her rich vocal nuance suggested a combination of seriousness and playfulness, fitting perfectly with the topic and purpose of the production. With energy and grace, her vocal performance transformed the mundane script into something more.

A huge spontaneous burst of applause from her peers nearly brought her to tears, as she reveled in the discovery of a talent she never knew she had. It was a sweet moment for her and for the whole class. When the video was posted online, Joyce proudly shared the link with her family and friends.

And what was even more surprising was that, immediately following this little production experience and for the rest of the semester, Joyce started to talk more often in class. Clearly more relaxed in front of her peers, she began to take some intellectual risks, trying out ideas and investing more as a participant in the discussions. Her peers began giving her more eye contact and even acknowledged her ideas on occasion. That little media production activity broke the ice that was keeping Joyce from being the best learner she could be.

As teachers, we must confront our own biases, preconceptions, stereotypes, and low expectations as we discover the capacities and talents of students who are struggling with school but who may have considerable competency at other skills, including things like vocal performance, video editing, graphic design, music composition, computer programming, or sound engineering.

In one memorable story, educator and scholar David Bruce remembers blanching when he saw the names of the boys on his high school roster list—these kids were real hockey pucks, as we say in Boston. But when Mr. Bruce invited his students to analyze media texts that were personally meaningful to them, the hockey pucks flourished. These were the boys with the lowest grades and the worst reputations. But when analyzing music and movies, these students could engage in a peer-led discussion. He writes as follows:

> As they read the lyrical and musical text of their selected song, they had a complex conversation, including offering textual support from the lyrics in informing their own interpretations and ideas. In a typical discussion over a classroom text, how often do teachers ask—or even beg—students to provide textual evidence for their ideas? These students demonstrated this skill as they composed a new video text.

Bruce concludes by pointing out that "numerous students who have not achieved school-defined success can engage in intelligent reading of and writing with video."[14]

In looking for ways to address the dropout problem we have in the United States, we must tap into the potential of media analysis and composition activities to reduce the achievement gap that's plaguing both urban and rural public schools.

Responsive Teaching

As we have seen in this book, good teachers have a set of shared competencies and values. They

- *Activate students' prior knowledge.* Teachers celebrate and respect student life and media experience, their interests and passions, and their understanding of the world.
- *Use digital media, mass media, and popular culture* to build knowledge and critical thinking skills, not as forms of entertainment or reward.
- *Are attuned to the teachable moment.* Teachers create focused learning goals and yet are open to new directions, capitalizing fully on the teachable moment that happens when a situation in the classroom makes for an opportunity to have an unexpected "Aha!" moment for learners.
- *Provide structure and scaffolding.* Teachers provide clear structure to learning tasks to ensure students' success and provide assistance and support to help a student become successful.
- *Ask "why" questions.* Teachers model the practice of questioning assumptions, encouraging students to dig deeper and verbalize their reasoning. They avoid being the "sage on the stage" and

dispensing wisdom in favor of helping students to acquire knowledge, solve problems, and think for themselves.

- *Value well-reasoned, independent thinking.* Teachers value diverse interpretations and points of view while insisting upon the use of reasoning, argument, and evidence to support interpretation.
- *Use collaborative multimedia composition to produce authentic communication.* Learners work together to compose new messages using media genres and forms that are appropriately challenging and meaningful for them to share their ideas with real audiences.
- *Respect learners.* Teachers create a climate for creativity to thrive, an open, playful, well-ordered, and respectful space for student learning.
- *Honor the learning process.* Teachers help students take pride in their work and support opportunities for students to be successful through repeated practice and revision.
- *Use authentic assessment.* Teachers use a range of strategies to measure students' growth and development with meaningful tasks and activities.
- *Participate as citizens of the world.* Teachers participate in self-governance as citizens themselves. They share their own curiosity and engagement with what's happening in their communities, the global village, and their subject areas. They take action as appropriate to address social problems.
- *Build a sense of community.* Teachers create a receptive community of learners, where everyone feels responsible for each other, offering authentic feedback that challenges us and helps us to grow.

Media texts and technology tools provide all of us, young and old, with resources for a lifetime of learning and entertainment—and they both represent and shape our culture's values and priorities, offering us a daily array of tensions and taboos.

When teachers have a set of conceptual principles, grounded in research evidence, it can guide instructional practices when using mass media and popular culture as tools for teaching and learning. Teachers learn how to select meaningful media texts for use in the classroom and how to recognize and use the teachable moment in dialogue and discussion about mass media and popular culture. This book has offered concepts and ideas to help you steer the ship.

Endnotes

Chapter 1

1. Nielsen. (2009, June). How teens use media: A Nielsen report on the myths and realities of teen media trends. Retrieved from http://blog.nielsen .com/nielsenwire/reports/nielsen_howteensusemedia_june09.pdf

2. Hobbs, R. (2006). Non-optimal use of video in the classroom. *Learning, Media, Technologies, 31*, 35–50.

3. National Council for the Social Studies. (2009, February). Position statement on media literacy. Retrieved from http://www.socialstudies.org/positions/medialiteracy1

4. Kaiser Family Foundation. (2010). Generation M2: Media in the lives of 8- to 18-year-olds. Retrieved from http://www.kff.org/entmedia/mh012010pkg.cfm

5. Salmond, K., & Purcell, K. (2011, February 9). Trends in teen communication and social media use: What's really going on here? Pew Internet and American Life Project. Retrieved from http://www.pewinternet.org/Presentations/2011/Feb/PIP-Girl-Scout-Webinar.aspx

6. Nielsen. (2009, June). How teens use media: A Nielsen report on the myths and realities of teen media trends. Retrieved from http://blog.nielsen .com/nielsenwire/reports/nielsen_howteensusemedia_june09.pdf

7. Gentile, D. A., & Walsh, D. A. (2002). A normative study of family media habits. *Applied Developmental Psychology 23*, 157–178.

8. Hobbs, R. (2010). *Digital and media literacy: A plan of action* (Knight Commission on the Information Needs of Communities in a Democracy). Washington, DC: Aspen Institute and Knight Foundation.

9. Ito, M., Baumer, S., Bittanti, M., Boyd, D., Cody, R., Herr-Stephenson, B., . . . Tripp, L. (2010). *Hanging out, messing around, and geeking out: Kids living and learning with new media.* (John D. and Catherine T. MacArthur Foundation Series on Digital Media and Learning). Cambridge, MA: MIT Press.

10. Shepherd, R. (1993, October/November).Why teach media literacy? *Teach Magazine.* Retrieved from http://www.media-awareness.ca/english/resources/educational/teaching_backgrounders/media_literacy/why_teach_shepherd.cfm

11. The term "essential question" was first introduced by Grant Wiggins and the Coalition of Essential Schools in the 1980s.

12. Scholes, R. (1995). An overview of Pacesetter English. *The English Journal, 84*(1), 69–75. (p. 69).

13. Hicks, T. (2009). *The digital writing workshop.* Portsmouth, NH: Heinemann.

14. Dewey, J. (1950). *Democracy and education.* New York: Macmillan. (Original work published 1916)

15. Ravitch, D., as cited in Lancto, C. (2003). *Banned books: How schools restrict the reading of young people.* Retrieved from http://www.worldandi .com/newhome/public/2003/september/mt2pub.asp

16. Argarwal, A. (2009, September 3). Data storage for user generated content. Retrieved from http://www.labnol.org/internet/data-storage-for-user-generated-content/9656/

17. Purcell-Gates, V., Duke, N., K., & Martineau, J. A. (2007). Learning to read and write genre-specific text: Roles of authentic experience and explicit teaching. *Reading Research Quarterly, 42*(1), 8–45.

18. Hobbs, R. (1998). The seven great debates in the media literacy movement. *Journal of Communication, 48*(1), 16–32.

Chapter 2

1. MTV. *16 and Pregnant.* Retrieved from Stay Teen: The National Campaign. Retrieved from http://www.stayteen.org/tuned/16-and-pregnant/default.aspx

2. McLane, M. N. (2007). The crucible: What's at stake in the sex-ed wars. *Boston Review, 32*(1), 27–30.

3. Love, M., & Helmbrect, B. (2007). Teaching the conflicts: (Re)engaging students with feminism in a postfeminist world. *Feminist Teacher, 18*(1), 41–58.

4. Love, M., & Helmbrect, B. (2007). Teaching the conflicts: (Re)engaging students with feminism in a postfeminist world. *Feminist Teacher, 18*(1), 41–58. (p. 58).

5. Buckingham, D. (2004). *Media education: Literacy, learning and contemporary culture.* London: Polity Press. (p. 16).

6. Pungente, J., Duncan, B., & Andersen, N. (2005). The Canadian experience: Leading the way. In G. Schwartz & Pamela U. Brown (Eds.), *Media literacy: Transforming curriculum and teaching* (104th Yearbook of the National Association for the Study of Education, Part I; pp. 140–160). Malden, MA: Blackwell.

7. Alvermann, D. E., Hagood, M. C., & Williams, K. B. (2001, June). Image, language, and sound: Making meaning with popular culture texts. *Reading Online, 4*(11). Retrieved from http://www.readingonline.org/newliteracies/lit_index .asp?HREF=/newliteracies/action/alvermann/index.html

8. Alvermann, D. E., Hagood, M. C., & Williams, K. B. (2001, June). Image, language, and sound: Making meaning with popular culture texts. *Reading Online, 4*(11). Retrieved from http://www.readingonline.org/newliteracies/lit_index.asp?HREF=/newliteracies/action/alvermann/index.html

9. Benson, S. (2010). I don't know if that would be English or not. *Journal of Adolescent and Adult Literacy, 53*(7), 555–563. (p. 560).

10. Postman, N. (1969, November). *Bullshit and the art of crap-detection.* Paper presented at the conference of the National Council of Teachers of English, Washington, DC. Retrieved from http://criticalsnips.wordpress .com/2007/07/22/neil-postman-bullshit-and-the-art-of-crap-detection

11. Postman, N. (1970). The politics of reading. *Harvard Educational Review, 40*, 244–252. (p. 11).

12. Moje, E. B., & Hinchman, K. (2004). Culturally responsive practices for youth literacy learning. In J. Dole & T. Jetton (Eds.), *Adolescent literacy research and practice* (pp. 331–350). New York, NY: Guilford Press.

13. Leinhardt, G. , Beck, I., & Stainton, C. (1994). *History: A time to be mindful* (pp. 209–255). Hillsdale, NJ: Lawrence Erlbaum.

14. Cheney, D. (2010). Fuzzy logic: Why students need news and information literacy skills. *Youth Media Reporter, 6*, 1. Retrieved from http://www.youthmediareporter.org/2010/06/fuzzy_logic_why_students_need.html

15. Walters, P., & Kop, R. (2009). Heidegger, digital technology and post-modern education: From being in cyberspace to meeting on My Space. *Bulletin of Science, Technology and Society, 29*, 278–286. (p. 285).

16. Kristin Cavallari says drugs were faked for show ratings. (2010). Anything Hollywood. Retrieved from http://anythinghollywood.com/2010/07/kristin-cavallari-drugs-faked-show-ratings

17. McRel. (2010). *Content knowledge* (4th ed.). Retrieved from http://www.mcrel.org/standards-benchmarks

18. Sisti, D. (2007). How do high school students justify Internet plagiarism? *Ethics and Behavior, 17*(3), 215–231.

19. Dant, D. (1986). Plagiarism in high school: A survey. *The English Journal, 75*(2), 81–84.

20. Kletzien, S. (2009). Paraphrasing: An effective comprehension strategy. *The Reading Teacher, 63*(1), 73–77.

21. Harris, F. (2008). Challenges to teaching credibility assessment in contemporary schooling. In M. Metzger & A. Flanagan (Eds.), *Digital media, youth and credibility* (The John D. and Catherine T. MacArthur Foundation Series on Digital Media and Learning; pp. 155–179). Cambridge, MA: MIT Press.

22. Metzger, M. J. (2007). Making sense of credibility on the web: Models for evaluating online information and recommendations for future research. *Journal of the American Society for Information Science and Technology, 58*(13), 2078–2091.

23. Sunstein, C. (2009). *On rumors.* New York: Farrar, Straus & Giroux.

24. Eysenbach, G., & Kohler, C. (2002). How do consumers search for and appraise health information on the World Wide Web? Qualitative study using focus groups, usability tests, and in-depth interviews. *British Medical Journal, 324*, 573–577.

Chapter 3

1. New Trier High School. (n.d.). American studies. Retrieved from http://www.newtrier.k12.il.us/page.aspx?id=818

2. This student blog entry from the 2009–2010 academic year has been removed from the website.

3. Masterman, L. (1985). *Teaching the media.* London: Comedia. (p. 19).

4. Jenkins, H., Puroshotma, R., Clinton, K., Weigel, M., & Robison, A. (2005). *Confronting the challenges of participatory culture: Media education for the 21st century.* Retrieved from http://www.newmedialiteracies.org/files/working/NMLWhitePaper.pdf

5. Postman, N., & Weingatner, C. (1969). *Teaching as a subversive activity* (pp. 33–35). New York, NY: Delacorte Press.

6. Buckingham, D. (2004). *Media education. Literacy, learning and contemporary culture.* London: Polity Press.

7. Hobbs, R. (2007). *Reading the media: Media literacy in high school English.* New York, NY: Teachers College Press.

8. Wilson, E. (2010, July 17). Informal remarks at the Aspen Institute Forum on Communications and Society, Aspen, CO.

9. Bonnett, M. (2002). Education as a form of the poetic: A Heideggerian approach to learning and the teacher-pupil relationship. In M. Peters (Ed.), *Heidegger, education and modernity* (pp. 229–244). Oxford, UK: Rowman & Littlefield. (p. 241).

Chapter 4

1. Caruso, E. M., Mead, N. L., & Balcetis, E. (2009). Political partisanship influences perception of biracial candidates' skin tone. *Proceedings of the National Academy of Sciences of the United States of America, 106*(48), 20168–20173.

2. Wiggins, G., & McTighe, J. (2006). *Understanding by design.* Upper Saddle River, NJ: Pearson Education. See also Wineburg, S. (2001). *Historical thinking and other unnatural acts: Charting the future of teaching the past.* Philadelphia, PA: Temple University Press.

3. Postman, N. (1969, November). *Bullshit and the art of crap-detection.* Paper presented at the conference of the National Council of Teachers of English, Washington, DC. Retrieved from http://criticalsnips.wordpress.com/2007/07/22/neil-postman-bullshit-and-the-art-of-crap-detection

4. Masterman, L. (1985). *Teaching the media.* London: Comedia. (p. 63).

5. Virginia Department of Education. (2008), Standards of learning, Virginia and U.S. history. Retrieved from http://www.doe.virginia.gov/testing/sol/standards_docs/history_socialscience/index.shtml

6. Virginia Department of Education. (2008), Standards of learning, Virginia and U.S. history. Retrieved from http://www.doe.virginia.gov/testing/sol/standards_docs/history_socialscience/index.shtml

7. Voelker, D. J. (2008). Assessing student understanding in introductory courses: A sample strategy. *The History Teacher, 41*(4), 505–518. (pp. 515–516). Retrieved from http://www.historycooperative.org/journals/ht/41.4/voelker.html

Chapter 5

1. Bradley, D. (2008). Scientific stereotype. *Sciencebase: Science News and Views.* Retrieved from http://www.sciencebase.com/science-blog/scientific-stereotype.html

2. Rensberger, B. (2000, July). The nature of evidence. *Science, 289,* 61.

3. Yerrick, R., Ross, D., & Molebash, P. (2003). Promoting equity with digital video. *Learning and Leading With Technology, 31*(4), 16–19.

4. Burn, A., & Durran, J. (2007). *Media literacy in schools: Practice, production and progression.* London: Paul Chapman. (p. 135).

5. Goble, D. (2009). Unique access to learning. Retrieved from http://www.ladue.k12.mo.us/lhwhs/teacher_websites/dgoble/don_iweb/Site/Unique_Access_Article.html

6. Smagorinsky, P. (2002). *Teaching English through principled practice.* Upper Saddle River, NJ: Merrill Prentice Hall. (p. 10).

7. Berry, J. (n.d.). *Conversations in science: Antiloguous harmony in chemistry and music* [Video]. Retrieved from http://mediaprodweb.madison.k12.wi.us/node/378

8. Whitehead, A. N. (1929). *The aims of education and other essays.* London: Williams and Norgate. (p. 31).

9. Whitehead, A. N. (1929). *The aims of education and other essays.* London: Williams and Norgate. (p. 27).

10. Roscoe, J., & Hight, C. (2001). *Faking it: Mock documentary and the subversion of reality.* Manchester, UK: Manchester University Press.

11. Metz, A. (2008). A fantasy made real: The evolution of the subjunctive documentary on U.S. cable science channels. *Television & New Media, 9,* 333–348.

12. Metz, A. (2008). A fantasy made real: The evolution of the subjunctive documentary on U.S. cable science channels. *Television & New Media, 9,* 333–348. (p. 344).

13. Barnett, M., & Kafka, A. (2007). Using science fiction movie scenes to support critical analysis of science. *Journal of College Science Teaching, 36*(4), 31–35.

14. Berger, J. (2007, May 2). Deciding when student writing crosses the line. *The New York Times,* p. 1. Retrieved from http://www.nytimes.com/2007/05/02/education/02education.html

15. Beaty, L. M. (2003, April). *The technology of video production, classroom practices and the development of a student voice in a changing world.* Paper presented at the conference of the American Educational Research Association, Chicago, IL.

16. Buckingham, D., & Sefton-Green, J. (1991). *Cultural studies goes to school.* London: Taylor & Francis. (p. 258).

17. Buckingham, D., & Sefton-Green, J. (1991). *Cultural studies goes to school.* London: Taylor & Francis. (p. 258).

18. Buckingham, D., & Sefton-Green, J. (1991). *Cultural studies goes to school.* London: Taylor & Francis. (p. 258).

19. Garcia, F., Kilgore, J., Rodriguez, P., & Thomas, S. (1995). "It's like having a metal detector at the door": A conversation with students about voice. *Theory Into Practice, 34*(2), 138–144. (p. 142).

20. Hazelwood v. Kuhlmeier, 484 U.S. 260 (1988).

21. Student Press Law Center. (2010). The 24/7 school day: Webcam lawsuit alleges new level of "creepiness." Retrieved from http://www.splc.org/wordpress/?cat=26

22. Beaty, L. M. (2003, April). *The technology of video production, classroom practices and the development of a student voice in a changing world.* Paper presented at the conference of the American Educational Research Association, Chicago, IL.

23. Kohn, A. (1986). *No contest: The case against competition*. Boston: Houghton Mifflin.

24. Ringrose, D. M. (2001). Beyond amusement: Reflections on multimedia, pedagogy, and digital literacy in the history seminar. *The History Teacher, 34*(2), 209–228. (p. 216).

Chapter 6

1. Downes, L. (2006, December 29). Middle school girls gone wild. *The New York Times*, p. 1. Retrieved from http://www.nytimes.com/2006/12/29/opinion/29fri4.html?scp=3&sq=Downes+girls+gone+wild&st=nyt

2. Brown, J., Halpern, C., & L'Engle, K. (2005). Mass media as a sexual super peer for early maturing girls. *Journal of Adolescent Health, 36*(5), 420–427.

3. Hargreaves, D. (2002). Idealized women in TV ads make girls feel bad. *Journal of Social and Clinical Psychology, 21*, 287–308.

4. American Association for Aesthetic Plastic Surgery. (2010). Teens and plastic surgery. Retrieved from http://www.surgery.org/media/news-releases/teens-and-plastic-surgery

5. Shippen, M. E., Houchins, D. E., Puckett, D., & Ramsey, M. (2007). Preferred writing topics of urban and rural middle school students. *Journal of Instructional Psychology, 34*(1), 59–66.

6. Jussell, A. (2007). Kids are a captive audience with ambient advertising. Retrieved from http://www.shapingyouth.org/?p=335

7. Lopez, S. (2007, March 18). *Billboard*'s Captivity audience disgusted. *Los Angeles Times*.

8. Oswell, D. (2008). Media and communications regulation and child protection: An overview of the field. In K. Drotner & S. Livingstone (Eds.), *The international handbook of children, media and culture* (pp. 475–492). London: Sage. (p. 476).

9. Davis, G. (2010). When gender equality is no longer a fairy tale. American Forum Op-Ed. Retrieved from http://amforumbacklog.blogspot.com/2010/06/when-gender-equality-is-no-longer-fairy.html

10. Whedon, J. (2007, May 20). Let's watch a girl get beaten to death. Whedonesque. Retrieved from http://whedonesque.com/comments/13271

11. Gauntlett, D. (2008). *Media, gender and identity*. London: Routledge. (p. 72).

12. Wasko, J. (2008). The commodification of youth culture. In K. Drotner & S. Livingstone (Eds.), *The international handbook of children, media and culture* (pp. 460–474). London: Sage. (p. 462).

13. Manjoo, F. (2008, July 21). Things are not what they stream. *Slate*. Retrieved from http://www.slate.com/id/2195687/

14. Kenway, J., & Bullen, E. (2001). *Consuming children: Education, entertainment, advertising*. London: Open University Press. (p. 153).

15. Kellner, D., & Share, J. (2007). Critical media literacy, democracy and the reconstruction of education. In D. Macedo & S. Steinberg (Eds.), *Media literacy: A reader*. New York, NY: Peter Lang. (pp. 3–23).

16. Healthy Within. (n.d.). Girl talk. Retrieved from http://www.healthywithin.com/Girl%20Talk.htm

17. Ramasubramanian, S., & Oliver, M. B. (2007). Activating and suppressing hostile and benevolent racism: Evidence for comparative media stereotyping. *Media Psychology, 9*(3), 623–646.

18. Kenway, J., & Bullen, E. (2001). *Consuming children: Education, entertainment, advertising.* London: Open University Press. (p. 153).

19. Buckingham, D., & Sefton-Green, J. (1994). *Cultural studies goes to school.* London: Taylor & Francis. (p. 38).

20. Masterman, L. (1985). *Teaching the media.* London: Comedia. (p. 24).

Chapter 7

1. Jenkins, H., with Purushotma, R., Weigel, M., Clinton, K., & Robison, A. J. (2009). *Confronting the challenges of participatory culture: Media education for the 21st century* (The John D. and Catherine T. MacArthur Foundation Series on Digital Media and Learning). Cambridge: MIT Press. (p. 12).

2. O'Connor, M. (2009). School speech in the Internet age: Do students shed their rights when they pick up a mouse? *University of Pennsylvania Journal of Constitutional Law, 11*(2), 459–486. (p. 484).

3. Gaudin, S. (2010, July 12). Women say they're increasingly addicted to Facebook. *Computerworld.* Retrieved from http://www.computerworld .com/s/article/9179100/Women_say_they_re_increasingly_addicted_to_ Facebook

4. Smith, Z. (2010, November 25). Generation why? *The New York Review of Books*, p. 3.

5. Mann, M. (1986). *The sources of social power.* Cambridge, UK: Cambridge University Press.

6. Staksrud, E., & Livingstone, S. (2009). Children and online risk. *Information, Communication & Society, 12*(3), 364–387.

7. Wolak, J., Mitchell, K. J., & Finkelhor, D. (2006). *Online victimization of youth: Five years on.* Durham, NH: University of New Hampshire, National Center for Missing & Exploited Children.

8. Staksrud, E., & Livingstone, S. (2009). Children and online risk. *Information, Communication & Society, 12*(3), 364–387. (p. 381).

9. Cheng, J. (2007, November 20). Top typo-squatted sites target children, some with porn. Ars Technica. Retrieved from http://arstechnica .com/old/content/2007/11/top-typo-squatted-sites-target-children-some- with-porn.ars

10. Ybarra, M., & Mitchell, K. (2005). Exposure to Internet pornography among children and adolescents: A national survey. *Cyberpsychology and Behavior, 8*(5), 473–486.

11. Bower, B. (2006, June 17). Growing up online. *Science News, 169,* 376–378.

12. Saroglou, V., & Anciaux, L. (2004). Liking sick humor: Coping styles and religion as predictors. *Humor, 17*(3), 257–278.

13. The Fred YouTube videos are so popular among young people that he has appeared on the Nickelodeon shows, *iCarly* and *Hannah Montana.*

14. Livingstone, S., & Thumim, N. (2008). What is Fred telling us? A commentary on youtube.com/fred. Retrieved from http://eprints.lse.ac.uk/23923

15. Hall, S. (2003). The spectacle of the Other. In S. Hall (Ed.), *Representation: Cultural representations and signifying practices* (pp. 223–290). London: Sage. (p. 258).

16. Flager, J. (1960, December 10). Profile: Student of the spontaneous. *The New Yorker*, 59. (p. 59).

17. McEntire, N. C. (2002). Purposeful deceptions of the April fool. *Western Folklore, 61*(2), 133–151.

18. Röcke, W., & Velten, H. R. (2005). *Lachgemeinschaften. Kulturelle Inszenierungen und soziale Wirkungen von Gelächter im Mittelalter und in der Frühen Neuzeit* [Communities of laughter: Cultural production and social effects of laughter in the middle ages and early modern period]. New York, NY: De Gruyter.

19. Nadis, F. (2007). Citizen Funt: Surveillance as Cold War entertainment. *Film and History, 37*(2), 13–22. (pp. 17–18).

20. Ziv, A. (1984). *Personality and sense of humor.* New York, NY: Springer.

21. Ferri, A. (2007). *Willing suspension of disbelief: Poetic faith in film.* Lanham, MD: Lexington Books.

22. Hobbs, R. (2008, May 25). Instant message, instant girlfriend. *The New York Times*, p. 6.

23. Hobbs, R. (2008, May 25). Instant message, instant girlfriend. *The New York Times*, p. 6.

Chapter 8

1. Urbina, I. (2010, March 24). Mobs are born as word grows by text message. *The New York Times*, p. 1.

2. Bogost, I., Ferrari, S., & Schweizer, B. (2010). *Newsgames: Journalism at play.* Cambridge, MA: MIT Press. (p. 126).

3. Personal interview with John Landis, July 26, 2010, Philadelphia, PA.

4. Rheingold, H. (2008). Using participatory media and public voice to encourage civic engagement. In L. Bennett (Ed.), *Civic life online: Learning how digital media can engage youth* (pp. 97–118). Cambridge, MA: MIT Press. (p. 104).

5. Brink, S. (2006, November 13). Prime time to learn. *Los Angeles Times*, p. 2.

6. Kaiser Family Foundation. (2002). Survey snapshot: The impact of TV's health content: A case study of ER viewers. Retrieved from http://www.kff.org/entmedia/3230-index.cfm

7. McManus, J. H. (2009). *Detecting bull.* Retrieved from http://www.detectingbull.com

8. Bennett, L. (2008). Changing citizenship in the digital age. In L. Bennett (Ed.), *Civic life online: Learning how digital media can engage youth* (pp. 1–24). Cambridge, MA: MIT Press.

9. Bennett, L. (2008). Changing citizenship in the digital age. In L. Bennett (Ed.), *Civic life online: Learning how digital media can engage youth* (pp. 1–24). Cambridge, MA: MIT Press. (p. 16).

10. Rheingold, H. (2008). Using participatory media and public voice to encourage civic engagement. In L. Bennett (Ed.), *Civic life online: Learning how digital media can engage youth* (pp. 97–118). Cambridge, MA: MIT Press.

11. Partnow, J. (2010, June). Media and news literacy in Seattle. *Youth Media Reporter, 6*(6). Retrieved from http://www.youthmediareporter .org/2010/06/media_and_news_literacy_in_sea.html

12. Partnow, J. (2010, June). Media and news literacy in Seattle. *Youth Media Reporter, 6*(6). Retrieved from http://www.youthmediareporter .org/2010/06/media_and_news_literacy_in_sea.html

13. Pulitzer Center on Crisis Reporting. (2010). Retrieved from http:// pulitzercenter.org

14. Jarman, R., & McClune, B. (2002). A survey of the use of newspapers in science instruction by secondary teachers in Northern Ireland. *International Journal of Science Education, 24*(10), 997–1020.

15. Houston, J. B., Pfefferbaum, B., & Reyes, G. (2008). Experiencing disasters indirectly: How traditional and new media disaster coverage impacts youth. *The Prevention Researcher, 15,* 14–17. (p. 17).

16. Levine, P. (2006). A public voice for youth. In L. Bennett (Ed.), *Civic life online: Learning how digital media can engage youth* (MacArthur Foundation Series; pp. 119–138). Cambridge, MA: MIT Press. (p. 121).

17. Deuze, M. (2006). Global journalism education. *Journalism Studies, 7*(1), 19–34.

18. Filak, V. F., Reinardy, S., & Maksl, A. (2009). Expanding and validating applications of the "willing to self-censor" scale. *Journalism & Mass Communication Quarterly, 86*(2), 368–382.

19. Harris, P. (2007). Solving the money problem in a television production class. *Technology Teacher, 66*(5), 22–28. (p. 26).

20. Cheifetz, G. (Director). (2006). *No child* [Youth documentary film]. Sixth Annual Media That Matters Film Festival. Retrieved from http:// www.mediathatmattersfest.org/films/no_child

21. Dunsmore, K., & Lagos, T. (2008). Politics, media and youth: Understanding political socialization via video production in secondary schools. *Learning, Media and Technology, 33*(1), 1–10. (p. 8).

22. Moore, D. C. (2011, March 4). *Trolling, transgression and cyberbullying in the classroom and at home.* Paper presented at the Digital Media and Learning Conference, Long Beach, CA.

23. Newspaper Association of America Foundation. (2010). NIE in 2010 = Leaner + Locally Focused + Digital. Retrieved from http://www.naafoun dation.org/Research/Foundation/NIE/NIE-in-2010.aspx

24. Kincheloe, J. L. (2001). *Getting beyond the facts: Teaching social studies/ social sciences in the twenty-first century.* New York, NY: Peter Lang.

25. Walker, T. R. (2010), as quoted in Kincheloe, J. L. (2001). *Getting beyond the facts: Teaching social studies/social sciences in the twenty-first century.* New York, NY: Peter Lang.

Chapter 9

1. Borthwick, A., Hansen, R., Gray, L., & Ziemann, I. (2008). Exploring essential conditions: A commentary on Bull et al. (2008). *Contemporary Issues in Technology and Teacher Education, 8*(3), 195–201. Retrieved from http:// www.citejournal.org/vol8/iss3/editorial/article2.cfm

2. Hobbs, R. (1998). The seven great debates in the media literacy movement. *Journal of Communication, 48*(2), 9–29.

3. Kress, G. (1992). Media literacy as cultural technology in the age of transcultural media. In C. Bazalgette, E. Bevort, & J. Savino (Eds.), *New directions: Media education worldwide* (p. 200). London: British Film Institute.

4. Hobbs, R. (2007). *Reading the media: Media literacy in high school English.* New York, NY: Teachers College Press.

5. Valenza, J. (2009, September 27). 14 ways K–12 librarians can teach social media. *Tech & Learning.* Retrieved from http://www.techlearning .com/article/23558

6. Peck, D., Clausen, R., Vilberg, J., Meidl, C., & Murray, O. (2009). *Classrooms for the Future (CFF): Year three evaluation report.* Harrisburg, PA: Pennsylvania Department of Education.

7. Smith, E. (2006). *Student learning through Wisconsin school library media centers: Library media specialist survey report.* Madison, WI: Wisconsin Department of Public Instruction, Division for Libraries, Technology and Community Learning.

8. Carbonaro, W., & Gamoran, A. (2002). The production of achievement inequality in high school English. *American Educational Research Journal, 39*(4), 801–882. (p. 805).

9. DeGennaro, D. (2010). Grounded in theory: Immersing preservice teachers in technology-mediated learning. *Contemporary Issues in Technology and Teacher Education, 10*(3), 338–359. Retrieved from http://www.citejournal .org/vol10/iss3/currentpractice/article1.cfm

10. Student Press Law Center. (1997). Student press protests policy. Retrieved from http://www.splc.org/news/report_detail.asp?id=198&edition=9

11. Fisher, D., & Frey, N. (2008). Doing the right thing with technology. *English Journal, 97*(6), 38–42.

12. Hobbs, R. (2006). Non-optimal use of video in the classroom. *Learning, Media, Technologies, 31*, 35–50.

13. Frey, N. (2008). Censorship and censorship policy: The impact of teaching literacy through the visual arts. In J. Flood, S. B. Heath, & D. Lapp (Eds.), *Handbook of teaching literacy through the communicative and visual arts* (Vol. II, pp. 65–72). Mahwah, NJ: Lawrence Erlbaum.

14. Bruce, D. (2008). Visualizing literacy: Building bridges with media. *Reading & Writing Quarterly, 24*, 264–282. (p. 280).

Bibliography

Alvermann, D. E., Hagood, M., & Williams, K. B. (2001, June). Image, language, and sound: Making meaning with popular culture texts. *Reading Online, 4*(11). Retrieved from http://www.readingonline.org/newliteracies/lit_index.asp?HREF=/newliteracies/action/alvermann/index.html

American Association for Aesthetic Plastic Surgery. (2010). Teens and plastic surgery. Retrieved from http://www.surgery.org/media/news-releases/teens-and-plastic-surgery

Argarwal, A. (2009, September 3). Data storage for user generated content. Retrieved from http://www.labnol.org/internet/data-storage-for-user-generated-content/9656

Barnett, M., & Kafka, A. (2007). Using science fiction movie scenes to support critical analysis of science. *Journal of College Science Teaching, 36*(4), 31–35.

Beaty, L. M. (2003, April). *The technology of video production, classroom practices and the development of a student voice in a changing world.* Paper presented at the conference of the American Educational Research Association, Chicago, IL.

Bennett, L. (2008). Changing citizenship in the digital age. In L. Bennett (Ed.), *Civic life online: Learning how digital media can engage youth* (pp. 1–24). Cambridge: MIT Press.

Benson, S. (2010). I don't know if that would be English or not. *Journal of Adolescent and Adult Literacy, 53*(7), 555–563.

Berger, J. (2007, May 2). Deciding when student writing crosses the line. *The New York Times*, p. 1. Retrieved from http://www.nytimes.com/2007/05/02/education/02education.html

Berry, J. (n.d.). *Conversations in science: Antiloguous harmony in chemistry and music* [Video]. Retrieved from http://mediaprodweb.madison.k12.wi.us/node/378

Bogost, I., Ferrari, S., & Schweizer, B. (2010). *Newsgames: Journalism at play.* Cambridge: MIT Press.

Bonnett, M. (2002). Education as a form of the poetic: A Heideggerian approach to learning and the teacher-pupil relationship. In M. Peters (Ed.), *Heidegger, education, and modernity* (pp. 229–244). Oxford, UK: Rowman & Littlefield.

Borthwick, A., Hansen, R., Gray, L., & Ziemann, I. (2008). Exploring essential conditions: A commentary on Bull et al. *Contemporary Issues in Technology and Teacher Education, 8*(3), 195–201. Retrieved from http://www.citejournal.org/vol8/iss3/editorial/article2.cfm

Bower, B. (2006, June 17). Growing up online. *Science News, 169,* 376–378.

Bradley, D. (2008). Scientific stereotype. *Sciencebase: Science News and Views.* Retrieved from http://www.sciencebase.com/science-blog/scientific-stereotype.html

Brink, S. (2006, November 13). Prime time to learn. *Los Angeles Times,* p. 2.

Brown, J., Halpern, C., & L'Engle, K. (2005). Mass media as a sexual super peer for early maturing girls. *Journal of Adolescent Health, 36*(5), 420–427.

Bruce, D. (2008). Visualizing literacy: Building bridges with media. *Reading & Writing Quarterly, 24,* 264–282.

Buckingham, D. (2004). *Media education: Literacy, learning and contemporary culture.* London: Polity Press.

Buckingham, D., & Sefton-Green, J. (1994). *Cultural studies goes to school.* London: Taylor & Francis.

Burn, A., & Durran, J. (2007). *Media literacy in schools: Practice, production and progression.* London: Paul Chapman.

Carbonaro, W., & Gamoran, A. (2002). The production of achievement inequality in high school English. *American Educational Research Journal, 39*(4), 801–882.

Caruso, E. M., Mead, N. L., & Balcetis, E. (2009). Political partisanship influences perception of biracial candidates' skin tone. *Proceedings of the National Academy of Sciences of the United States of America, 106*(48), 20168–20173.

Cheifetz, G. (Director). (2006). *No child* [Youth documentary film]. Sixth Annual Media That Matters Film Festival. Retrieved from http://www.mediathatmattersfest.org/films/no_child

Cheney, D. (2010). Fuzzy logic: Why students need news and information literacy skills. *Youth Media Reporter, 6,* 1. Retrieved from http://www.youthmediareporter.org/2010/06/fuzzy_logic_why_students_need.html

Cheng, J. (2007). Top typo-squatted sites target children, some with porn. *Ars Technica.* Retrieved from http://arstechnica.com/old/content/2007/11/top-typo-squatted-sites-target-children-some-with-porn.ars

Dant, D. (1986, February). Plagiarism in high school: A survey. *The English Journal, 75*(2), 81–84.

Davis, G. (2010). When gender equality is no longer a fairy tale. *American Forum Op-Ed.* Retrieved from http://amforumbacklog.blogspot.com/2010/06/when-gender-equality-is-no-longer-fairy.html

DeGennaro, D. (2010). Grounded in theory: Immersing preservice teachers in technology-mediated learning. *Contemporary Issues in Technology and Teacher Education, 10*(3), 338–359. Retrieved from http://www.citejournal.org/vol10/iss3/currentpractice/article1.cfm

Deuze, M. (2006). Global journalism education. *Journalism Studies, 7*(1), 19–34.

Dewey, J. (1950). *Democracy and education.* New York: Macmillan. (Original work published 1916)

Downes, L. (2006, December 29). Middle school girls gone wild. *The New York Times,* p. 1. Retrieved from http://www.nytimes.com/2006/12/29/opinion/29fri4.html?scp=3&sq=Downes+girls+gone+wild&st=nyt

Dunsmore, K., & Lagos, T. (2008). Politics, media and youth: Understanding political socialization via video production in secondary schools. *Learning, Media and Technology, 33*(1), 1–10.

Eysenbach, G., & Kohler, C. (2002). How do consumers search for and appraise health information on the World Wide Web? Qualitative study using focus groups, usability tests, and in-depth interviews. *British Medical Journal, 324,* 573–577.

Ferri, A. (2007). *Willing suspension of disbelief: Poetic faith in film.* Lanham, MD: Lexington Books.

Filak, V. F., Reinardy, S., & Maksl, A. (2009). Expanding and validating applications of the "willing to self-censor" scale. *Journalism & Mass Communication Quarterly, 86*(2), 368–382.

Fisher, D., & Frey, N. (2008). Doing the right thing with technology. *English Journal, 97*(6), 38–42.

Flager, J. (1960, December 10). Profile: Student of the spontaneous. *The New Yorker,* p. 59.

Frey, N. (2008). Censorship and censorship policy: The impact of teaching literacy through the visual arts. In J. Flood, S. B. Heath, & D. Lapp, (Eds.), *Handbook of teaching literacy through the communicative and visual arts* (Vol. 2, pp. 65–72). Mahwah, NJ: Lawrence Erlbaum.

Garcia, F., Kilgore, J., Rodriguez, P., & Thomas, S. (1995). "It's like having a metal detector at the door": A conversation with students about voice. *Theory Into Practice, 34*(2), 138–144.

Gaudin, S. (2010, July 12). Women say they're increasingly addicted to Facebook. *Computerworld.* Retrieved from http://www.computerworld .com/s/article/9179100/Women_say_they_re_increasingly_addicted_ to_Facebook

Gauntlett, D. (2008). *Media, gender and identity.* London: Routledge.

Gentile, D. A., & Walsh, D. A. (2002). A normative study of family media habits. *Applied Developmental Psychology, 23,* 157–178.

Goble, D. (2009). Unique access to learning. Retrieved from http://www .ladue.k12.mo.us/lhwhs/teacher_websites/dgoble/don_iweb/Site/ Unique_Access_Article.html

Goodman, P. (2008, December 3). A shopping Guernica captures the moment. *The New York Times,* p. 3.

Hall, S. (2003). The spectacle of the Other. In S. Hall (Ed.), *Representation: Cultural representations and signifying practices* (pp. 223–290). London: Sage.

Hargreaves, D. (2002). Idealized women in TV ads make girls feel bad. *Journal of Social and Clinical Psychology, 21,* 287–308.

Harris, F. (2008). Challenges to teaching credibility assessment in contemporary schooling. In M. Metzger & A. Flanagan (Eds.), *Digital media, youth, and credibility* (The John D. and Catherine T. MacArthur Foundation Series on Digital Media and Learning; pp. 155–179). Cambridge: MIT Press.

Harris, P. (2007). Solving the money problem in a television production class. *Technology Teacher, 66*(5), 22–28.

Hazelwood v. Kuhlmeier, 484 U.S. 260 (1988).

Healthy Within. (n.d.). Girl talk. Retrieved from http://www.healthywithin .com/Girl%20Talk.htm

Hicks, T. (2009). *The digital writing workshop.* Portsmouth, NH: Heinemann.

Hobbs, R. (1998). The seven great debates in the media literacy movement. *Journal of Communication, 48*(1), 9–29.

Hobbs, R. (2006). Non-optimal use of video in the classroom. *Learning, Media, Technologies, 31,* 35–50.

Hobbs, R. (2007). *Reading the media: Media literacy in high school English.* New York: Teachers College Press.

Hobbs, R. (2010). *Digital and media literacy: A plan of action.* Knight Commission on the Information Needs of Communities in a Democracy. Washington, DC: Aspen Institute and Knight Foundation.

Hobbs, R. J. (2008, May 25). Instant message, instant girlfriend. *The New York Times,* p. 6.

Houston, J. B., Pfefferbaum, B., & Reyes, G. (2008). Experiencing disasters indirectly: How traditional and new media disaster coverage impacts youth. *The Prevention Researcher, 15,* 14–17.

Ito, M., Baumer, S., Bittanti, M., Boyd, D., Cody, R., Herr-Stephenson, B., et al. (2010). *Hanging out, messing around, and geeking out: Kids living and learning with new media.* John D. and Catherine T. MacArthur Foundation Series on Digital Media and Learning. Cambridge: MIT Press.

Jarman, R., & McClune, B. (2002). A survey of the use of newspapers in science instruction by secondary teachers in Northern Ireland. *International Journal of Science Education, 24*(10), 997–1020.

Jenkins, H., Purushotma, R., Clinton, K., Weigel, M., & Robison, A. (2005). *Confronting the challenges of participatory culture: Media education for the 21st century.* Retrieved from http://www.newmedialiteracies.org/files/working/NMLWhitePaper.pdf

Jenkins, H., with Purushotma, R., Weigel, M., Clinton, K., Robison, A. J. (2009). *Confronting the challenges of participatory culture: Media education for the 21st century.* The John D. and Catherine T. MacArthur Foundation Reports on Digital Media and Learning. Cambridge: MIT Press.

Jussell, A. (2007). Kids are a captive audience with ambient advertising. *Shaping Youth.* Retrieved from http://www.shapingyouth.org/?p=335

Kaiser Family Foundation. (2002). *Survey snapshot: The impact of TV's health content: A case study of ER viewers.* Retrieved from http://www.kff.org/entmedia/3230-index.cfm

Kaiser Family Foundation. (2010). *Generation M2: Media in the lives of 8- to 18-year-olds.* Retrieved from http://www.kff.org/entmedia/mh012010pkg.cfm

Kellner, D., & Share, J. (2007). Critical media literacy, democracy, and the reconstruction of education. In D. Macedo & S. Steinberg (Eds.), *Media literacy: A reader* (pp. 3–23). New York: Peter Lang.

Kenway, J., & Bullen, E. (2001). *Consuming children: Education, entertainment, advertising.* London: Open University Press.

Kincheloe, J. L. (2001). *Getting beyond the facts: Teaching social studies/social sciences in the twenty-first century.* New York: Peter Lang.

Kletzien, S. (2009). Paraphrasing: An effective comprehension strategy. *The Reading Teacher, 63*(1), 73–77.

Kohn, A. (1986). *No contest: The case against competition.* Boston: Houghton Mifflin.

Kress, G. (1992). Media literacy as cultural technology in the age of transcultural media. In C. Bazalgette, E. Bevort, & J. Savino (Eds.), *New directions: Media education worldwide.* London: British Film Institute.

Kristin Cavallari says drugs were faked for show ratings. (2010). Anything Hollywood. Retrieved from http://anythinghollywood.com/2010/07/kristin-cavallari-drugs-faked-show-ratings

Leinhardt, G. (1994). History: A time to be mindful. In G. Leinhardt, I. Beck, & C. Stainton (Eds.), *Teaching and learning in history* (pp. 209–255). Hillsdale, NJ: Lawrence Erlbaum.

Levine, P. (2006). A public voice for youth. In L. Bennett (Ed.), *Civic life online: Learning how digital media can engage youth* (MacArthur Foundation Series; pp. 119–138). Cambridge: MIT Press.

Livingstone, S., & Thumim, N. (2008). What is Fred telling us? A commentary on youtube.com/fred. Retrieved from http://eprints.lse.ac.uk/23923

Love, M., & Helmbrect, B. (2007). Teaching the conflicts: (Re)engaging students with feminism in a postfeminist world. *Feminist Teacher, 18*(1), 41–58.

Manjoo, F. (2008, July 21). Things are not what they stream. *Slate.* Retrieved from http://www.slate.com/id/2195687

Mann, M. (1986). *The sources of social power.* Cambridge, UK: Cambridge University Press.

Masterman, L. (1985). *Teaching the media.* London: Comedia.

McEntire, N.C. (2002). Purposeful deceptions of the April Fool. *Western Folklore, 61*(2), 133–151.

McLane, M. N. (2007). The crucible: What's at stake in the sex-ed wars. *Boston Review, 32*(1), 27–30.

McManus, J. H. (2009). *Detecting bull.* Retrieved from http://www.detectingbull.com

McRel. (2010). *Content knowledge* (4th ed.). Retrieved from http://www.mcrel.org/standards-benchmarks

Metz, A. (2008). A fantasy made real: The evolution of the subjunctive documentary on U.S. cable science channels. *Television & New Media, 9,* 333–348.

Metzger, M. J. (2007). Making sense of credibility on the web: Models for evaluating online information and recommendations for future research. *Journal of the American Society for Information Science and Technology, 58*(13), 2078–2091.

Moje, E. B., & Hinchman, K. (2004). Culturally responsive practices for youth literacy learning. In J. Dole & T. Jetton (Eds.), *Adolescent literacy research and practice* (pp. 331–350). New York: Guilford Press.

Moore, D. C. (2011, March 4). Trolling, transgression and cyberbullying in the classroom and at home. Presentation at the Digital Media and Learning Conference, Long Beach, CA.

MTV. *16 and Pregnant.* Retrieved from http://www.stayteen.org/tuned/16-and-pregnant/default.aspx

Nadis, F. (2007). Citizen Funt: Surveillance as Cold War entertainment. *Film and History, 37*(2), 13–22.

National Council for the Social Studies. (2009, February). Position statement on media literacy. Retrieved from http://www.socialstudies.org/positions/medialiteracy

Newspaper Association of America Foundation. (2010). NIE in 2010 = Leaner + Locally Focused + Digital. Retrieved from http://www.naafoundation.org/Research/Foundation/NIE/NIE-in-2010.aspx

New Trier High School. (n.d.). American studies. Retrieved from http://www.newtrier.k12.il.us/page.aspx?id=818

Nielsen. (2009, June). How teens use media: A Nielsen report on the myths and realities of teen media trends. Retrieved from http://blog.nielsen.com/nielsenwire/reports/nielsen_howteensusemedia_june09.pdf

O'Connor, M. (2009). School speech in the Internet age: Do students shed their rights when they pick up a mouse? *University of Pennsylvania Journal of Constitutional Law, 11(2)*, 459–486.

Oswell, D. (2008). Media and communications regulation and child protection: An overview of the field. In K. Drotner & S. Livingstone (Eds.), *The international handbook of children, media and culture* (pp. 475–492). London: Sage.

Partnow, J. (2010, June). Media and news literacy in Seattle. *Youth Media Reporter, 6(6)*. Retrieved from http://www.youthmediareporter.org/2010/06/media_and_news_literacy_in_sea.html

Peck, D., Clausen, R., Vilberg, J., Meidl, C., & Murray, O. (2009). *Classrooms for the Future (CFF): Year three evaluation report.* Harrisburg, PA: Pennsylvania Department of Education.

Postman, N. (1969, November). *Bullshit and the art of crap-detection.* Paper presented at the conference of the National Council of Teachers of English, Washington, DC. Retrieved from http://criticalsnips.wordpress.com/2007/07/22/neil-postman-bullshit-and-the-art-of-crap-detection

Postman, N. (1970). The politics of reading. *Harvard Educational Review, 40*, 244–252.

Postman, N., & Weingartner, C. (1969). *Teaching as a subversive activity.* New York: Delacorte Press.

Pulitzer Center on Crisis Reporting. (2010). Retrieved from http://pulitzercenter.org

Pungente, J., Duncan, B., & Andersen, N. (2005). The Canadian experience: Leading the way. In G. Schwartz & Pamela U. Brown (Eds.), *Media literacy: Transforming curriculum and teaching* (104th Yearbook of the National Association for the Study of Education, Part I; pp. 140–160). Malden, MA: Blackwell.

Purcell-Gates, V., Duke, N. K., & Martineau, J. A. (2007). Learning to read and write genre-specific text: Roles of authentic experience and explicit teaching. *Reading Research Quarterly, 42(1)*, 8–45.

Ramasubramanian, S., & Oliver, M. B. (2007). Activating and suppressing hostile and benevolent racism: Evidence for comparative media stereotyping. *Media Psychology, 9(3)*, 623–646.

Ravitch, D., as cited in Lancto, C. (2003). *Banned books: How schools restrict the reading of young people.* Retrieved from http://www.worldandi.com/newhome/public/2003/september/mt2pub.asp

Rensberger, B. (2000, July). The nature of evidence. *Science, 289*, 61.

Rheingold, H. (2008). Using participatory media and public voice to encourage civic engagement. In L. Bennett (Ed.), *Civic life online: Learning how digital media can engage youth* (pp. 97–118). Cambridge: MIT Press.

Ringrose, D. M. (2001). Beyond amusement: Reflections on multimedia, pedagogy, and digital literacy in the history seminar. *The History Teacher, 34(2)*, 209–228.

Röcke, W., & Velten, H. R. (2005). *Lachgemeinschaften. Kulturelle Inszenierungen und soziale Wirkungen von Gelächter im Mittelalter und in der Frühen Neuzeit* [Communities of laughter: Cultural production and social effects of laughter in the Middle Ages and early modern period]. Berlin/New York: De Gruyter.

Roscoe, J., & Hight, C. (2001). *Faking it: Mock documentary and the subversion of reality.* Manchester, UK: Manchester University Press.

Salmond, K., & Purcell, K. (2011, February 9). *Trends in teen communication and social media use: What's really going on here?* Pew Internet and American Life Project. Retrieved from http://www.pewinternet.org/Presentations/2011/Feb/PIP-Girl-Scout-Webinar.asp

Saroglou, V., & Anciaux, L. (2004). Liking sick humor: Coping styles and religion as predictors. *Humor, 17*(3), 257–278.

Scholes, R. (1995). An overview of Pacesetter English. *The English Journal, 84*(1), 69–75.

Shepherd, R. (1993, October/November).Why teach media literacy? *Teach Magazine.* Reprinted with permission at http://www.media-awareness.ca/english/resources/educational/teaching_backgrounders/media_literacy/why_teach_shepherd.cfm

Shippen, M. E., Houchins, D. E., Puckett, D., & Ramsey, M. (2007). Preferred writing topics of urban and rural middle school students. *Journal of Instructional Psychology, 34*(1), 59–66.

Sisti, D. (2007). How do high school students justify Internet plagiarism? *Ethics and Behavior, 17*(3), 215–231.

Smagorinsky, P. (2002). *Teaching English through principled practice.* Upper Saddle River, NJ: Merrill Prentice Hall.

Smith, E. (2006). *Student learning through Wisconsin school library media centers: Library media specialist survey report.* Madison, WI: Wisconsin Department of Public Instruction, Division for Libraries, Technology and Community Learning.

Smith, Z. (2010, November 25). Generation why? *The New York Review of Books,* p. 3.

Staksrud, E., & Livingstone, S. (2009). Children and online risk. *Information, Communication & Society, 12*(3), 364–387.

Student Press Law Center. (1997). Student press protests policy. Retrieved from http://www.splc.org/news/report_detail.asp?id=198&edition=9

Student Press Law Center. (2010). The 24/7 school day: Webcam lawsuit alleges new level of "creepiness." Retrieved from http://www.splc.org/wordpress/?cat=26

Sunstein, C. (2009). *On rumors.* New York: Farrar, Straus & Giroux.

Urbina, I. (2010, March 24). Mobs are born as word grows by text message. *The New York Times,* p. 1.

Valenza, J. (2009). 14 ways K–12 librarians can teach social media. *Tech & Learning.* Retrieved from http://www.techlearning.com/article/23558

Virginia Department of Education. (2008). *Standards of learning, Virginia and U.S. history.* Retrieved from http://www.doe.virginia.gov/testing/sol/standards_docs/history_socialscience/index.shtml

Voelker, D. J. (2008). Assessing student understanding in introductory courses: A sample strategy. *The History Teacher, 41*(4), 505–518. Retrieved from http://www.historycooperative.org/journals/ht/41.4/voelker.html

Walters, P., & Kop, R. (2009). Heidegger, digital technology, and postmodern education: From being in cyberspace to meeting on My Space. *Bulletin of Science, Technology and Society, 29,* 278–286.

Wasko, J. (2008). The commodification of youth culture. In K. Drotner & S. Livingstone (Eds.), *The international handbook of children, media and culture* (pp. 460–474). London: Sage.

Whedon, J. (2007, May 20). Let's watch a girl get beaten to death. Whedonesque. Retrieved from http://whedonesque.com/comments/13271

Whitehead, A. N. (1929, 1946). *The aims of education and other essays.* London: Williams and Norgate.

Wiggins, G., & McTighe, J. (2006). *Understanding by design.* Upper Saddle River, NJ: Pearson Education.

Wilson, E. (2010, July). Aspen Institute Forum on Communications and Society, Aspen, CO.

Wineburg, S. (2001). *Historical thinking and other unnatural acts: Charting the future of teaching the past.* Philadelphia, PA: Temple University Press.

Wolak, J., Mitchell, K. J., & Finkelhor, D. (2006). *Online victimization of youth: Five years on.* Durham, NH: University of New Hampshire, National Center for Missing & Exploited Children.

Ybarra, M., & Mitchell, K. (2005). Exposure to Internet pornography among children and adolescents: A national survey. *Cyberpsychology and Behavior, 8*(5), 473–486.

Yerrick, R., Ross, D., & Molebash, P. (2003). Promoting equity with digital video. *Learning and Leading With Technology, 31*(4), 16–19.

Ziv, A. (1984). *Personality and sense of humor.* New York: Springer.

Index

CORWIN
A SAGE Company

The Corwin logo—a raven striding across an open book—represents the union of courage and learning. Corwin is committed to improving education for all learners by publishing books and other professional development resources for those serving the field of PreK–12 education. By providing practical, hands-on materials, Corwin continues to carry out the promise of its motto: **"Helping Educators Do Their Work Better."**